Inside Out

INSIDE OUT

An Autobiography by a Native Canadian

James Tyman

Fifth House Publishers
Saskatoon, Saskatchewan

Because many of the events discussed in this book are quite recent, some names have been changed.

Canadian Cataloguing in Publication Data

Tyman, James, 1963-
Inside out:the autobiography of a Native Canadian
ISBN: 0-920079-49-0
1. Tyman, James, 1963-. 2. Métis-Biography *.
I. Title
FC109.1.T963A3 1989 971/.00497 C89-098121-3
E99.M693T963 1989

This book was published with the assistance of The Saskatchewan Arts Board and The Canada Council.

Design: Robert MacDonald, MediaClones Inc.
Saskatoon Saskatchewan, Banff Alberta and Toronto Ontario

Printed and bound in Canada

Fifth House Publishers
20–36th Street East
Saskatoon, SK
S7K 5S8

PART ONE
Racism

The smell of spilled wine, whisky, beer, and unwashed bodies stung the nostrils. But if you had lived there long enough the smell was natural. It infested your clothes and hair, the food, the furniture. It was as common to this household as the odor of frying bacon was to thousands of other households across Canada every morning.

"Watch what you're doing, Kenny!"

"I am."

"Damn kid!" The huge man jumped to his feet, spilling the bottle of whisky he kept by him night and day. "I'll teach you to talk back!" He threw the boy to the couch, pressing one knee on his chest. "Quit your crying! You baby!" The beating lasted long enough to knock the child unconscious. "There! Now you aren't so smart, are you!" The man walked back to the table. He cursed at the sight of the spilled whisky. "See what you made me do!" He went to the kitchen and retrieved a half bottle he had left over from last night. He poured himself a glass. "C'mon, you baby! Get up! Start cleaning up around here!" But my father was too drunk to realize I was still unconscious.

I imagined this scene countless times as I tried to picture what horrible things had happened to cause my mother to let the Saskatchewan Social Services Department take me away. I have been told that on one occasion my father nearly took my life. My name then was Kenny Howard Martin. I was the youngest of five sons and three daughters. I have no memories of the beatings and the abuse. I've blocked out everything from those days.

I learned of my father's violence and abuse years later when I finally met my mother in a downtown bar. It was a bar frequented by prostitutes, pimps, drug dealers and their customers, winos, ex-cons, perverts of every persuasion, people running from the law. My mother was not one of these. She drank there because it was where she was accepted for what she was — an Indian, like most of the other patrons. This was her place of refuge, her place to be with her own. She had been a part of the human misery that so many of the other patrons had also been a part of.

When she gave me a history of my toddler years, it helped me understand why I did the things I did, and why I thought I was nuts, and different from the people I grew up with. But the story really begins the day I walked into my new home in Fort Qu'Appelle, Saskatchewan, a scared and lonely four-year-old, toting all my personal possessions in a suitcase the same size as me.

SEPTEMBER 1967

Who is this woman? Where is she taking me? Am I going to die? Somebody said I would do the world a favor if I died. Death is where you go to sleep and have peace forever. It sounds inviting. It's got to be better than what I feel.

"Come along, Jimmy. This is your new home."

To a four year old it looks like a mansion. It's so clean. It has little stones all over the wall that sparkle. How do they do that? She called me Jimmy. My name isn't Jimmy. I want to tell her my name is ... I don't know. I'm standing in the porch. The huge brown table is full of white people. They look different. They stare at me like I'm different. I feel like crying. The adults are talking about me. "He'll do fine," the nice-looking lady says. "Fine," I say to myself. I think she means I'm okay. What am I okay for? My body feels sick and lonely, and awfully scared. I'm afraid of these men. The oldest one, soon to be my father, is smiling at me. The two young men just stare, then resume eating. They're going to be my brothers. The four girls smile at each other. Are they laughing at me?

"Come Jimmy, I'll show you to your room," the woman says kindly. I follow her. Women have been kind to me, men have scared me. My head is bowed when she talks to me. I just want to go home. Where is home? I know these are not my family. Why am I here? The social worker said the Tymans would look after me and give me all the love I need. What's love? But she said it so gently. I wanted this love. I know fear. I cry when I get scared. I feel like crying now. She is pleasant, but those men, they scare me.

I was so quiet the first few days that I would startle people, coming up behind them. I sat for hours in my new room, peeking out at the Tymans. If they turned toward me, I would scoot away. I was afraid that if I didn't listen to them I would be beaten.

I had nightmares about being helpless. I would see "him" coming. I couldn't run from "him." I would wake up, wide-eyed, clutching my blanket. I'd peek over at the closet in my room. It had sliding doors. Every time I jolted from sleep I swear they had opened another few inches. My nightmares were always about this man. He would grab me and throw me down a deep pit, laughing hysterically. Or he'd hold me under water, drowning me, and again I'd hear the sickening laughter. I always woke up in time. But he was there in that closet, waiting for me to fall back to sleep.

There was a time I wanted to go home. I wasn't sure where home was, but this was not my home. Once I went into the basement and climbed up into the crawl space by the wall. I thought I could keep crawling till I came out of this house and back to where I belonged. There were boxes of old clothes and shoes up there, and miscellaneous household articles. There was also a photo album, and something prompted me to look in there for my family. As I looked through the book it dawned on me that I didn't know who I was looking for.

The pleasant-looking woman and the man with the smile were worried about me. I could hear them calling "Jimmy, Jimmy!" I didn't answer. I crouched behind a cardboard box as I heard the father come down the stairs. I'm in trouble now. He's going to beat me. I watched him look around, calling "Jimmy." But he didn't look mean. As he was leaving the room I shouted, "I'm right here!"

"Why didn't you answer me?"

"I was just playing." I walked up to him, waiting for the beating.

"You had us worried." He placed his hand on my head. "Come upstairs, son."

Son! I looked up at him. He was smiling. I was confused. He didn't raise his voice, he didn't strike me. He called me "son." It felt good. I knew he wasn't Dad. But still, something inside me melted that day. I was beginning to feel this love that I'd heard of.

Before I started school, I spent the days with my mother. We went shopping together, and it was always thrilling when people I didn't know came up to us. I'd get my hair tousled and a warm smile. "This must be Jimmy. Oh, he is a darling." If I was lucky they'd give me candy. I noticed other Indian kids on these excursions. We'd stare at each other in fascination — I the nicely dressed young native with this white woman, and they with their stringy hair and worn clothes. Their parents looked just the same. Some of the men were loud and obnoxious. I studied them closely. There was something there I could almost remember. But the ones who were swaggering and abusive terrified me. I never wanted to run into them again. But I was beginning to understand what I was from these visits to the grocery store. They were dark-skinned, and so was I. The kids I played with were white and too young to care what I was, but sometimes one of them would ask me, "You're Indian, aren't you?"

I didn't know the difference, so I'd reply cheerfully, "Yeah."

"Your mom isn't."

I couldn't answer that. I would resume playing, and soon it would be forgotten. But when I was alone, the conversation would come back to me — "Your mom isn't" — and later I'd cry myself to sleep.

My mother had a friend who came over for coffee in the afternoons. Her daughter was a year older than me and a real tomboy. Anita and I became inseparable. Other boys teased me for playing with a girl. But I was more comfortable with Anita than with other town kids. I didn't like boys. My mother and her friend rationalized it this way: "Jimmy has two sisters near his age, and no little brothers to play with." It sounded good to me. Anita never once asked me about being Indian. In fact we used to joke about the stupid Indians with their dirty clothes and hair, sleeping in the tall weeds behind the hotel on Main Street. To her I was just a good friend, someone to play ball with, or wrestle, or watch cartoons with. But when the day was over I'd look in the mirror, and there was that same dark skin. What was wrong?

1969

The summer before my first year of school, I was terrified. I'd grown accustomed to the security of being with my mother. Now she said I'd make new friends and meet a nice teacher. I'd learned from Anita that there were thousands of kids at school. I didn't know how much thousands were, but it was too many for me. I'd learned from experience that other kids would call me Indian and ask questions I couldn't answer. The idea of going to school with thousands of these kids was frightening. Then one day the school bus came. It was going to take us to a town called Lebret, four miles away. But we lived right across the street from a school! My mother may have tried to explain why there was no grade one at this school, but I wasn't buying it. When the day came to go to Lebret, I panicked. I was being sent away again. I ran off the bus, crying hysterically.

"Please, Mommy, don't send me away!"

"Come, Jimmy, you'll make new friends there."

"No!"

I clutched her tightly. She walked me back to the bus. By this time the other kids all had their faces pressed to the windows, watching the little Indian being comforted by the white woman.

So here I am, sitting in a bus full of kids. I watch my mother walking away. I can feel everyone's eyes on me. I still have tears running down my face. I look around. There is someone else like me! He's dark-skinned. I wonder, though, why are his eyes slanted?

Now I'm sitting in a classroom full of gabby students. I feel scared and lonely again. My mom said I'm coming back for supper. I don't know what to believe. A couple of kids ask me what I was crying for. I give them a stare and bow my head. I want to go home.

"Good morning, class. I'm your teacher, Sister Campbell." She is smiling. "You may call me Miss Campbell."

"Sister," I tell myself. "I know you. You're the nun at the church my mom and dad take me to every Sunday."

I can relax now. Nothing will happen to me. Nuns are good people. She knows I'm here. She knows my mom and dad. She won't let me be sent away.

There was an Indian Residential School down the road in Lebret. It went around the schoolyard that if you were bad, the teachers would send you there. That terrified us because it was full of Indians. Conversations at recess molded my outlook toward them. Everything I heard was negative:

"I hear they have to beat the Indians, to get them to learn."

"My brother says Indians will steal your stuff."

The Residential School was more commonly referred to as a prison. When our bus drove by I found myself straining to see the gun towers, the barbed wire fence, the high cement wall. Then in the schoolyard I would sit and listen. Our school was across the street from our church. My teacher was in the choir.

The man at the piano with the beautiful voice was the principal of the Residential School. If the place was so bad, I wondered, why did he seem so nice? I saw only a few Indians attending church, though. My belief then was that if you didn't go to church you were going to hell, and only good people went to church. I concluded that Indians were bad people; they didn't go to church. No wonder my friends didn't like them. They were going to hell!

In Sunday School I learned to speak in hushed tones when talking about Jesus. My friends and I were afraid that if we got him mad, Jesus's father would zap us with a bolt of lightning. My mother was the Sunday School teacher, and I was proud to hear her talking about Jesus and all the magical things he did. We were given books about the biblical days. I would turn the brightly illustrated pages in fascination. Jesus could fly! Not only that, but anyone who died could fly. They floated around up in the clouds. Some were playing harps. They were always dressed in white. Another fascinating thing was that there were no Indians floating around in the clouds. In fact, there were no Indians at all in these books! Yes sirree, Indians were evil.

Once I got hold of a Swiss Army Knife, and I was playing with it in Sunday School. When my mother asked what I was doing, I thrust it into the air. "Just playing with my knife, Mom." The other kids jumped. My mother had a look of astonishment on her face. The next day I was questioned — in class, in the school ground, on the bus — about my brave, defiant act. I made new friends, and some kids stopped picking on me. I thought it was because they liked me.

When I finished my first year of school, my report card was full of VGs and EXs. I didn't know what that meant, but everyone was complimenting me. When I got off the bus my sisters looked at my card. "Ah Jim!" they said, "you did good." My mother was just as pleased, and everyone passed the card around. It was the best report card I ever had.

1970-1971

My second year in school would have been the same as the first, except that I made friends with a couple of farm boys. They were known as troublemakers. I'd noticed that they seemed to be popular with other students, and even at that age I felt I didn't belong. I wouldn't even have met them if I hadn't pulled out that knife in Sunday School. I always down-played the incident, but to them it was an act of defiance, and something to be admired. I didn't mind, I was making "cool" friends.

Even so, I was still fairly passive. One thing that kept me in line was the fact that the principal used to be in the army. He was never seen wearing anything but his army uniform. He had a reputation as a strict disciplinarian. He wasn't afraid of strapping your hand till it was crimson. He was never caught smiling, and there were a few times when the farm boys came back from his office with tears streaming down their cheeks. Looking back, though, I wish he had been my principal for another four or five years. Between his strict guidance at school and my father's at home, my behavior might have been different.

1972

I entered the new school year with a new attitude: I was going to be one of the boys, not just one of their lackeys. I followed through, too. Six of us got hauled down to the principal's office one day for bringing a gopher into the classroom. Another time we brought in garter snakes and let them loose in someone's desk. We were always pulling stunts like that, usually at my instigation. The teacher knew who was responsible, but I was always let off with warnings. I'd always been quiet and solitary, and they thought it was a good sign that I was coming out of my shell. My farm friends always took the brunt of the principal's wrath. One time five of us were sent to the office for discipline. The principal grabbed the others one by one, shaking them and yelling in their faces. I was shaking, I knew this fear. But he stopped at me and simply told me to smarten up. My accomplices asked why. We concluded that the principal must be scared of Indians.

I began to hate myself that year. I was getting teased by the white kids, and nothing I said seemed to matter. If I talked back it only made them taunt me more, until I just laughed along with them and then they would stop. But it hurt. I'd go home and look in the bathroom mirror and curse the color of my skin. Why couldn't I be like the other kids? My parents treated me with love, but at school I learned of the Indians and their savage ways, how they scalped people, how they'd tie you across an anthill till the insects ate you alive. It chilled me to the bone to think of such a horrible death. I wondered if that was what the Indians did out on the reservations that surrounded Fort Qu'Appelle. We'd sit in class telling horror stories about how the Indians were going to come in and burn the village and scalp everybody. "But they'll leave you alone, Jimmy," a snooty kid would announce. "You're one of them." I hated her for saying those things.

"My family is white."

"Doesn't matter. They bought you. You're an Indian."

I'd go home and scrub my hands, hoping to wash the darkness off.

If I agreed with them, they'd leave me alone. But I was hurting inside. And I was learning to hate them and myself for being Indian.

I can look back now and see what I was doing and why, but I never told anyone. I never asked my parents about these stories about Indians. They were white, of course they'd confirm the stories. And on TV the Indians were blood-thirsty savages killing the white settlers, and the cavalry would have to be sent in to stop them. "Red devils." Yes, Indians were going to hell. The TV would not lie.

I should have asked my parents.

After school I wandered around town looking at the Indians

and trying to figure out if what they said in school was true. They looked harmless enough, I thought. I knew I was an Indian, but according to my friends I didn't act like other Indians. What was an Indian supposed to act like? My mom and dad bought me? Could that be possible? I never asked them. I just kept it all inside.

1973

The next year we were back at Lebret for grades four through six. I was learning new things there. I was learning how to fight. And I was learning that the more you fought, the more other kids left you alone. I was also making friends with an Indian who was constantly the center of discussion, for his parents were known as the town drunks. We'd see the pair of them staggering wildly down the street and call out, "Have one for me!" They'd turn and wave happily. My friend would just stare at them in silence. I often wondered what he was thinking. My friend and his brothers were always skipping out of school. They were each suspended on separate occasions. One day we heard angry shouts from the hallway.

"You bitch! Kick my boy out? Who do you think you are? You damn honkies!" It was my friend's mother yelling face to face with my home-room teacher.

"You start sending your kids to school and they won't get kicked out!"

My home-room teacher was quite athletic and my friends's mother was rather large. All the kids were hoping for a fight. But soon the teachers were ushering us back to the classroom. We learned later that my friend's mother did take a swing at my teacher, but she was swiftly wrestled to the ground. The police came and took her away to sleep it off.

"Is that how your mother used to act, Tyman?" a kid asked. He had a group of friends backing him up, so I just smiled and said, "No, she'd have dropped the bitch right away." They all laughed, but I was hurting at the insult to my unknown mother, and with having to cover up my feelings. But expressing them only meant more and deeper insults about my heritage.

I was solitary once I got off the bus back in Fort Qu'Appelle. I'd wander around trying to put things in focus. I knew I'd been adopted, but from where? Who was my mom? I tried to remember, but all that came to me was walking in the Tymans' front door. Kids at school asked me where I came from. A few teachers did, too. "From under a rock," I'd answer cheerfully. They would laugh and the questions would stop.

The friendships I was developing then were with a bunch of new kids from the big city of Regina. The Hanson boys were shy by nature. The kids use to pick on them, calling them all sorts of clever names like dummy, air-head, and retard. I found myself attracted to these outcasts. I spoke to them on occasion, and they whispered their answers, hoping no one else heard them. Their names were Francis, Andrew, Phil, and there was an older brother named William. The family had countless arguments over the years — about me. Should I be allowed in their house? Their father was opposed to the idea. I wasn't sure why at first, but later it became obvious. The head of their family did not want an Indian hanging around his house and kids.

What a relationship. These boys were my best friends, and they had a father who'd rather have seen me dead than sitting in his front porch waiting for his sons to come out. He didn't want them roaming the town with this Indian. It was unthinkable, unholy. He threw me out of the house on a few occasions. Several times he banished me from his property forever, only to have his own sons protesting the injustice of it. I was used to racist slurs, but this man was simply not prepared to give me even one chance.

Our principal then was Mr Allan. What was interesting about this was that his son was another of my good friends, and like the city boys' father, the man did not like me one bit. If I spoke up when he was quizzing the class, he'd give me a poisonous stare. It didn't do my self-esteem much good, being disliked by the school principal. The kids tormented me about it. "Who cares?" I said. I was learning my tough-guy role, to stop the pain from showing. Even so, I didn't want to believe he disliked me because I was Indian. His son was quick to answer my doubts. "Dad doesn't like Indians," he laughed. "I think you're okay, though, Jim."

This was probably the reason I rebelled against school authority in the coming years. "He doesn't like Indians." Why? I wanted to tell my father and mother, but would they believe something I couldn't understand myself? I never asked.

Often in the mornings now I'd pretend I was sick, or damn near dying, trying to convince my mother to let me stay home. It got so bad that I'd eat 30 aspirins or so and of course I'd get one helluva gut ache and wouldn't have to fake it any more. I didn't care. I hated school, I hated the principal, I hated being Indian.

More and more Indian kids were coming to public schools at that time, and Lebret was getting its share. Some of these kids had been living on the reserve all their lives, and they hated honkies as much as honkies hated them. A lot of them would talk about how their big brother was in jail for beating somebody. "You pick on me and I'll tell my brother" was all anyone needed to hear. The kid was left alone.

"Is that where your mom and dad are, Tyman?"

"Probably, killed a whole bunch of honkies," I'd say, and they'd laugh. Here was a dilemma, though: the reserve Indians hated me because my friends were "white trash," as they put it, and most of the white kids hated me because I was a "scummy Indian." So I'd find my few friends and we'd avoid both the white racists and the warriors. Is this what life is all about? I wondered.

I used to escape alone sometimes. I'd get up early Saturday morning and jump on my bike and ride up to the hills surrounding Fort Qu'Appelle. I'd follow the cattle trails that ran through the bush. There was a dog that met me every Saturday morning, wagging his tail; it was like he was waiting for me. I'd greet him and off we'd go, across the hills on the cattle trails, always mindful of the droppings that littered our route, till we came to a clearing that overlooked the town. Those were some memorable moments, sitting up there with this dog, telling him my problems. I told him how people hate you because your skin is colored. "They'd be right confused with you," I used to say, because my little friend had brown patches over a predominantly white coat. He was the only one I could confide in. It helped, too. He seemed to understand. At least he didn't laugh.

We'd sit and watch the traffic pass on the highway to Regina. I told him how I wished I was in one of those cars. I didn't care where it went as long as it was away from this town. I was always having thoughts of running away. I tried to convince a couple of friends to come with me. I'd bring them down to the tracks, and when a train stopped to load grain from the elevator I'd tell them how easy it would be just to jump on the train and we'd be gone.

"But what will we eat, Jim?"

"We'll raid gardens."

"I don't know, Jim. It sounds like a bad idea. I love my family."

That always shut me up. I wanted to explain to them about my family. I didn't hate the Tymans. They gave me everything I needed, but it all seemed artificial, it wasn't real. I felt I was being looked after because someone had told them to, not because they wanted to. I was wrong about them. Racism hurt them, too. My older sister, Donna, had to put up with questions like, "How's the little Indian doing?" Or they'd compare me to black paint, just to get her mad.

I hate these people, I thought. They're all wrong about me. I'm just like them. I think like them. I eat like them. I have feelings like them. I can't help being who I am. I want to die. It came back to me: dying is where you go and have peace forever. I grabbed a knife. I figured with careful planning I could make it look like an accident. It had to look like an accident. It was my tough-guy role: I didn't want my school mates to know they'd won. I wanted it to look like I fell on the knife running up from the basement, a tragic accident. I don't know what kept me pulling the knife away every time I fell.

I watched a show on television that showed a woman slashing her wrists with a razor. That looked like it would work. I practiced. First I slashed my shins. Then the blood came out and the pain set in, and that was the last of that idea. I told my mom and dad that I'd cut myself on a barbed wire fence. Looking back, I'm grateful that my father wasn't a hunter. For sure I'd have found myself peering down the barrel of a loaded gun. "I know it won't hurt. Bang! Then it'll be all over." It would have been over all right.

My father and mother were mystified during these times, also. How could their son, who was so quiet and good at home, be the way the teacher described him at school? I was always ready to fight at school. I was always back-talking the teachers and being disruptive. I wanted them to tell me what was wrong with me. There was only one problem: I couldn't tell them what the problem was!

"What the hell is the matter with you?" my father shouted, clutching a dismal report from my teacher.

"Nothing's the matter." I bowed my head. I couldn't tell him why I hated school. He wouldn't understand. I tried to tell him about my relationship with the principal, but he was shocked at what I was suggesting. The principal a racist? I drew my conclusions: if my father and mother couldn't believe me about school ... well, they wouldn't believe the other stuff, either. Teachers did sit me down and ask me why I was being so abusive. I wanted to shout out the questions:

"Why don't people like my color?"

"Why do the Indians call me apple?"

"Why are my old school friends ignoring me now?"

But it was only to myself that I was shouting. So, like my mother and father, the teachers didn't know why this kid was being such a jerk. My behavior and reputation followed me through school. And these scenes repeated themselves, my parents protesting angrily at my behavior, the teachers and principal protesting angrily at my behavior. And every time they asked, "What is wrong with you?," I got tongue-tied. I wanted to confide in someone. There had to be someone who would understand what I was going through. To some I was an object of scorn, to others an object of pity. "I know you're adopted, Jim. My father feels sorry for you." Why? Is it so shameful to be adopted? "Who are your real parents, Jim?" That question was always there. I didn't know my real name, let alone my real parents.

1976

The bus was full of excited children as it pulled away from Lebret elementary school on June 28th, 1976 for the summer break. I was jubilant. "It's finally over," I whispered to myself in the back seat of the bus. I turned to watch my grade six teacher and our principal standing side by side on the lawn. One of my friends had said he was going to moon them and give them the finger.

"Hey, come here." I gestured to him.

"Yeah, what d'you want?" His breath smelled of cigarette smoke.

"You going to pull the moon?"

"Well, no. She passed me."

"Don't be a chicken."

He smiled and laughed. "Well ... no, but here, see." As the bus pulled away, he banged the glass and thrust his middle finger up. The teacher just nodded with a half grin on her face. The principal's face hardened, looking at me. Then came his familiar poisonous stare. We kept our eyes locked till the bus turned the corner and was climbing the hill to the highway.

The ride back to Fort Qu'Appelle took about 10 minutes. By the time those 10 minutes were over I had decided not to let the teachers intimidate me any more, and to seek physical confrontation with anyone who insulted me without cause. These convictions guided me through the remainder of my school years. I'd had enough emotional abuse from my schoolmates. They had insulted me, they had turned their back on me, and they had shamed me, all because I was Indian. When I was at Lebret and getting into fist fights, a group of white kids used to gather round me after school and try to hurt me. Sometimes I got lucky and a teacher would come by and put a stop to what I was sure was going to be my lynching. What was sad about these mob gatherings was that these were the same kids I used to be good friends with in my first years at school. Now I was shunned, and occasionally beaten up if I got caught in one of those gatherings. And I knew what lay ahead: high school. There I'd meet more scorn than Lebret could produce. It was easy to figure out, my classmates were getting tutored. They were "learning" about Indians from young men and women in the upper grades.

At that time my parents were building a new house on the outskirts of town. It was situated on a hill by the golf course, overlooking Fort Qu'Appelle and two lakes plus the south side of the valley hills. It was a remarkable view on a summer night, watching the glittering town lights a mile away down below, and the mirrored images off the lake from the cabin lights that ran 20 miles either side of Fort Qu'Appelle.

My father came home from his job as maintenance supervisor at the local hospital at five o'clock. As quickly as he could get into some work clothes, he and my mother would be off to work on the house. This house brought the Tyman family closer together, because the Tymans did everything but dig the basement and drill the well. It forged a special bond between family members. In later years it forged a special bond between my father and me, too, as we worked side by side putting the finishing touches on it. But before then I went through a period of transition.

What had happened at school was etched in my mind, and the racism seem to grow as fast as I did. Now when I ventured downtown only a few people said hello, or stopped to talk. I remembered when people used to tousle my hair when I was smaller. Now I was 12 years old and 170 pounds. By the time I was 15 I was five feet, 11 inches, and 200 pounds. It did make people less inclined to make snide remarks about my race or my unknown family, though.

Mom and Dad were always close by, but they were dead tired when they came home, and quickly went to bed. Weekends and holidays they were fully occupied with the new house. With the lax supervision, I was free to do what I wanted.

We were a middle-class family, so I made middle-class friends. We started our own gang, like most kids our age did. We were called the James Gang after one of our members decided to use my name when we got into a scuffle with the local hockey school. "We're the James Gang!" he shouted defiantly. I was mad at him for using my name, but it stuck. We were never very threatening to the public at large. We raided gardens, threw tomatoes and eggs at passing cars, stuff like that. You could say we were the good gang, because Fort Qu'Appelle had a bad gang. They were constantly trying to fight us. Their members were mostly Indians, and most of them went to jail by their 17th birthday — one for armed robbery, the rest for car thefts, assaults, break and enters and other petty crimes. One of their favorite tricks was to blame us for their deeds, which did nothing to help our reputations. But the police figured out who was behind most of the mischief around town as their members began telling on each other. One of the lessons I would learn in later years was never to trust a fellow thief.

Their leader lived down the street. At nights we'd be throwing rocks at each other from behind trees, and once I broke his sister's car window. Well, he couldn't get into the house fast enough to tell her. She came storming out.

"You little bastards are going to pay for that damn window! Do you hear me?"

"Blow it out your ass!"

"What did you say!" She was infuriated. She started to walk over to my yard. Bad mistake.

Rocks, tomatoes, anything we could throw flew off in her direction. She ran back to safety. Her brother and his friends took up the offensive, to the dismay of the neighbors. They often came storming out of the house, threatening to call the police, our parents, anybody who'd stop the melée.

We weren't the only ones who didn't like the bad gang. Under the cover of darkness one night, two of my sister's friends took a can of paint and proceeded to write all types of lovely slogans on the leader's new garage. Shortly after that I was approached by our local RCMP.

"Hey, Jim, why did you paint the garage?"

"You got the wrong guy."

He smiled broadly. "Who did it, then?"

"He probably did it himself, just to blame me."

His face didn't stop smiling. "Why would he do that?"

"'Cause ... I don't know. Go ask him."

"We did." He stopped smiling. "That's why we're talking to you."

I didn't say another word. We stared at each other in silence for a moment, then he motioned to the driver. "Watch yourself, Jim." The cruiser lurched forward and sped off.

It was my first contact with the police. It was the beginning of a long relationship.

* * *

I was alone in the house one Saturday afternoon when I got the impulse to enter my parents' bedroom. I knew they kept our old report cards there, and I wanted to see the kinds of things the teachers used to write about my two older brothers. I didn't think they'd had as much trouble in school as I was having, but I thought comparing my behavior with theirs might help me understand why I acted the way I did.

I was fumbling through some papers when I came across a

large brown envelope marked "Saskatchewan Social Services Department." My head went light. There was a letter with "Adopt Indian Métis" in dark blue letters across the top. I must be a Métis Indian, I thought. I wondered what tribe that was. I knew we had Sioux Indians all around us on the reserves. But where was the Métis reserve? I read on: "Born in Ile-à-la-Crosse, Saskatchewan." Where the hell was that? My mom said I was born in Saskatoon. The letter gave those two bits of vital information; the rest was details of meetings for parents to attend in Regina. I read it three times. There was no hint of who I was, no name. But its impact on me was staggering.

Up until then I'd felt very close to my mother and father. Now I felt alienated; it was a mixture of love and hate, and my resentment was building. I wanted to know who my biological mom was, but who could I ask? My adopted mother? I couldn't figure out why they'd never told me anything.

It took a few days for me to realize I should look in the encyclopedia for a map of Saskatchewan and find out where Ile-à-la-Crosse was. I flashed through the index. There it was! "Ile-à-la-Crosse, G-5." I put one finger on G and the other on 5. Ile-à-la-Crosse was 200 miles northwest of Saskatoon. One road went there, and according to the map that's where it ended. Ile-à-la-Crosse was the end of the road, the end of civilization. I shut the encyclopedia. I was more confused than ever. I was alone in the house, so I went back to the drawer which contained my past.

I looked through the letters from the Social Services Department. Again there were meetings for my parents to attend, and one letter listing all the diseases I'd contracted. It was a long list. I tried to remember being so sick. There were no names on these letters, just "the subject."

"I'm a subject," I smiled to myself. Then I finally found some news: "Kenny Howard Martin was placed with William and Cecile Tyman on September 17th, 1967. His new name will be James Kenneth Tyman." I felt a heat rush. That was it! Now I know who I am. I have another family. But where are they?

My mind flashed back to the day I walked into the Tymans' house, the time I hid up in the crawl space, the time my sister showed me how to ride a bike in the dusty street out front, which was now paved. I remembered the first bike the Tymans gave me: it was red and had training wheels. I smiled at that thought. I use to spend hours roaring around the house, almost running into my mom's afternoon visitors. I remembered all the questions the kids asked about my "real" family. Now I could tell them where I was born. I sat on the back fence mulling over my memories. They were pleasant, the ones about growing up in this home.

When Mom and Dad came home I watched them as they talked about their day's accomplishments at the new house. I wondered why they had taken me. I wondered why I had been put up for adoption. I wondered, more than anything, why I hadn't been told anything. That question was always with me. I'd say, "This is the day I ask what's going on." But I didn't know how to approach them. I thought, "If they didn't want to talk about it, then maybe I shouldn't bring it up." That was my reasoning. What it was, really, was my means of escaping what I concluded would be some pretty painful memories. Why else couldn't I remember a thing?

My emotions were in turmoil that summer. I felt cheated by a mother I didn't even know. I felt deserted. I felt angry because the Tymans hadn't told me the truth. I felt resentment toward people who gave me a hard time about who I was. What did they know? "No one cares about me!" I shouted out one day. "So I don't care about anyone!" I was walking through Valley Center Park, just below where my parents were constructing the house. I looked up and saw them working away. "Why you guys?" I asked myself.

I felt alienated from the Tymans and "their relatives," as I put it. I felt awkward at family gatherings. I stuck out like a sore thumb in family pictures. I wanted to talk, to ask questions. But I didn't want to rock the boat. The family members were in a jubilant mood most of the time, building their new home. It was my father's dream house. I didn't want to bring up such a sensitive subject and disrupt the harmony of the family. I kept it inside. My conflicting emotions were eating me up like a cancer.

1976-1978

At Bert Fox Composite High School in Fort Qu'Appelle, my home room was run by another nun, Sister Regina Anne. She liked to walk the hallway with the peace sign raised for everyone to see. She received all types of comments.

"Right on, Sis!"

"Tell it like is."

"Amen!"

"Hallelujah!"

Our home room was full of misfits and troublemakers. I had more and more contact with Indians. One of them, Lorne, was my tutor, so to speak. I approached him with humor at first: "You Indians scalp anyone on the reserve lately!"

He knew I was joking, but he was visibly upset by it. "We don't scalp people. How do you think we learned to scalp?"

"Skinning beavers and gophers," I shot back.

"You don't know too much, do you?" His face was bent in a scowl.

I quit smiling. "What d'you mean?"

"I mean, you're no Indian. You grew up with whiteys all your life. They taught you that we scalped people, right?"

"Well, that's the truth ... isn't it?"

He snickered lightly. "Pile of bullshit. Get some Indian bros. Quit hanging around with honkies. Maybe you'll see what the truth really is."

Hang around with Indians? He must be kidding.

"What type of Indian are you?" he questioned me.

"Métis! I'm a Métis Indian."

"So, you're one of them," he drawled. "Who's white? Your mom or your dad?"

I was puzzled. "What do you mean, who's white?"

Again he snickered, this time more loudly. "Shit, Tyman, you sure don't know much. A Métis is a half-breed, half Indian and half French. There's a lot of Métis Indians around. You heard of Riel?"

"Riel was a honky," I exclaimed.

"He looked like a honky, but he was the same as you. You're just the darker version."

"Darker version, hey." I felt a sense of relief then, not because I was actually sitting down talking to an Indian, but because I realized I was half white.

"Well, who's the French one?" he continued.

"I don't know. I'm adopted."

"Well, well." He was nodding his head. "That explains you."

"What do you mean by that?"

"It explains why you hang around with honkies all the time, and the way you act."

"What way is that?"

"You act like a clown, entertaining your honky friends all day. That's not really you. You're just acting that way to get their approval."

"I don't act like that!" I lied. "I'm just bored with school."

"Yeah, sure thing, Tyman." He leaned back in his chair. "You're just bored."

I turned around in my desk. Damn Indian, what does he know? I don't act for them, I just don't like school. I pinched the girl in front of me. She squealed. When the teacher looked up, I was innocently doing school work. My friends grinned. I was one of them.

My behavior in school got bad enough that in most classes I had my desk directly in front of the teacher's, where I could be kept under surveillance. It meant I had to think up sneakier tactics, or wait till the teacher left the room for a moment, so chaos could reign: erasers and pencils flew through the air, elastic sling-shots launched everything from spitballs to paper clips. It would continue until the teacher was just pushing the door open. We'd have set a garbage can in the way to cause a moment of confusion for the teacher, and allow us time to return to our school work.

I made a few trips to the principal's office that first year at BFCHS.

"You watch what you're doing, Tyman! I bloody well mean it! You think I'm joking?" He grabbed the front of my jacket and shook me. "You're pushing for a suspension! I won't hesitate to throw your wise ass out of here for a few days! Maybe a whole school year!" He glared menacingly at me. "Now get the hell out of here, and you better damn well stay out of my office!"

That was the way he operated. No explanation on your part was needed. He was a large man, six feet four inches and 250 pounds. It was intimidating to have him grab you by the collar and shake you like a rag doll, or to have him roar in your face for 20 minutes about conduct unbecoming to his fine high school. Usually after a session with him I watched what I did — for a while.

I started to enter the pool hall down on Main Street. It was mostly occupied by the town's "undesirables," as my teachers called them. A lot of gambling and drinking went on. A lot of drunks made the pool hall their daily stop. It was a hideout for kids skipping school. It was also a refuge for people who had already dropped out and simply needed a place to go. My friends the farm boys were right at home in this atmosphere. Their years in school were numbered, and they knew it. School to them was just a matter of doing time till they could legally quit "and be free," as they described it.

I was hanging around with the school's bad boys. Aside from the farm boys who were just putting in time, there was a small native kid who laughed at trivial things. He was always talking about marijuana and pills, and the "fuckin' honkies." He mentioned how he'd planned to commit suicide once, but all the pills he ate just made him throw up instead. Then he laughed hysterically. We told him how crazy he was to think of something like that, let alone try it. But my memories of attempted suicide came back to me, and I wondered if it was common for Indians to try to kill themselves so young.

Those were my friends back then. They were the ones who influenced me to use marijuana and sip whisky, and to start smoking cigarettes. My old school chums were learning the fine art of social climbing, and it was definitely not cool to be seen with an Indian.

* * *

Summer came and I breathed a sigh of relief. I spent more and more time by myself. I'd spend hours in the pool hall, playing pool, gambling, and occasionally sipping whisky from the local boozers who were growing accustomed to seeing me.

This was a hang-out for the Indians who came to town on a regular basis, too. Now, some of these boys did not like me at all. I was part of a white family, so it was cut and dried with them: I was a traitor. There were always some big boys who wanted to rearrange my boyish looks. But there were some other big boys who came to my defense whenever an incident was about to unfold in the street.

"I kicked that son of a bitch in the head last night!" a local unemployed man exclaimed to me the day after one of these incidents. Now, I only saw this guy occasionally, and he was 10 or 15 years older than me. I wondered who else was protecting me in the smoke-filled pool hall.

My Indian friend from school was a regular, too: "Hey, Tyman, where's your honky friends?"

"Shit, Lorne, you know they'd never come in here unless there was 10 of them."

"Smoke a joint, Tyman? Or are you still too white for that?"

"Still too white! Sure, I'll give it a try." I had tried smoking marijuana once before, with the boy who talked of suicide. I didn't like it, but it was a way of gaining acceptance and "being cool."

* * *

My father and I started to work together, putting the finishing touches on the house. I always grumbled when he wanted me to work Saturday afternoons when all the other kids would be heading to the beach. I wanted to be at the beach with them. It's true that I was generally feeling alienated from the community, but if I was with them at least they wouldn't forget me.

I had to stand in the hot sun mixing cement. My father made jokes at my grumbling, and told me to work harder. He used some pretty crude language those days. "Don't ever use this language in front of your mother," he'd warn me. Then after a hard day's work we'd walk the hills together. He would tell me stories from his past, or give me his philosophy on issues he knew I could understand. It made me feel he was treating me like a grown-up. I could tell he was trying to reach me. We grew closer, and I developed a deep respect for this man.

He could be stern and threatening, too, especially when he got another dismal report from my teachers about my attitude and behavior in class. "What the hell is your problem?" he would demand to know. "You'd better smarten up, boy, or you're never getting out of this house!"

His threatening approach would work for a while, because it terrified me. I couldn't shake those frightening feelings I had of getting beaten. Most kids would joke from time to time about their father giving them a licking. I couldn't. I'd be almost overcome with fear. I knew it wasn't normal for me to be so scared. I hated him for it, but I wouldn't tell him.

* * *

I was constantly looking for someone to fight with to release my growing fury. That I never got beat up myself was due to my insane behavior. Most kids would quit fighting after one of the combatants said he'd had enough. Not me. There were always a few kids jumping on my back. I thought they were trying to pile on me, but they were just trying to break up the fight. My mad approach to fist-fighting caused them to move in packs and isolate me even more. "He's too crazy," they said. But if you kick a dog and abuse it, if you surround him and throw rocks at him, day after day and week after week, that dog will more than likely grow up mean. Then if he bites you because you were one of the rock throwers, who is to blame?

I had another release besides fighting. I played floor hockey, and any other sport that demanded physical exertion. I played intensely, ramming people into the walls every chance I got. Of course this led to everyone else playing rough as well, and it usually ended with someone going down hurt. I got kicked off the floor on a regular basis for rough play. This disturbed me because I wasn't the only one getting rough out there. But the supervisor would give me a smug grin and tell me to get off the floor. I wasn't anyone's favorite student. But I became good at floor hockey, and people started to accept me more. It kept me from skipping out of school, because I liked to play in the regular games at noon hour, and it was always good to be sitting in the change room afterward with people congratulating me on a good game. There were always the die-hards, though — "Not bad for an Indian" — and another fight would start.

As time went on people learned that I got upset if they made snide remarks about my being Indian. It may have stopped a few fights, but it started a few also.

"Hey, look at the breed."

I turned to face the older kid. He was in grade 11. His parents owned a grocery store in town. The sound of my fist echoed through the hallway as it landed square between his eyes. He staggered back, then came at me. I caught him twice more, on the eye and lip. Then the Industrial Arts teacher separated us, and we were led down to face the principal.

"What the hell is going on with you two!" the principal was not having voice problems. "Marchuck, you should know better, you're older!"

"He just turned and hit me." It sounded pretty feeble.

"That's bullshit. He called me a breed!"

"Watch your language, Tyman! I don't believe you! You're always causing problems!" The principal turned toward Marchuck. "You better not have any more incidents like this with the younger students, Marchuck! Do I make myself clear?"

"Yes sir." Marchuck bowed his head. What a phony.

"You're treading on thin ice, Tyman! Now both of you get out of my office!"

Jilted again. The principal didn't care if people called me down. He wouldn't believe me. To hell with him.

I was always getting into trouble with the kids of parents who were well off. What is odd about this was, I often got along with their parents. They were all smiles when they met me in the street. The first job I got out of school was with Marchuck's dad, who praised my performance.

1979

I was now 15 years old, and the last few years had distanced me more than ever; there was no more fellowship with my old school chums. They'd talk to me in school but that was it. Come the weekend I was out of the picture. I had a few good times with the Hanson boys, but their father was coming down on them hard for being my friend. He'd rant and rave about me when they sat down for supper. The boys would tell me this, and I felt guilty that I was the cause of such bad feelings. They told me how the family was divided. Where I had once been friends with all the boys, I was only friends with two now, and all the time they would be speaking in my defense. I hated their father.

They were constantly getting into scrapes with the "in crowd," as a certain group considered themselves. The in crowd labeled the Hanson boys idiots and retards. I was angry with the in crowd, as they took it on themselves to approve or reject anyone new in the school. The Hansons had been around for years, but they were still shunned because of their quiet manner and disposition. Eventually the rejection took its toll: only one graduated, the rest quit. But even the city boys and I didn't see eye to eye on a few occasions.

"I want to get a gun and shoot all the Indians!" one of them exclaimed one day.

"Shoot all the Indians! What about me?"

"Oh, not you, Jim. You're a good Indian."

I was elated that he saw me as a good Indian. There were a lot of bad Indians in town, as I learned from reading the court briefs in the newspaper. The majority of people going to jail were from the reserves around town. I didn't want people to look at me and think I was one of them.

In the meantime I have a couple of new friends — both of them dropouts, both of them darker than me. They share something in common with me: rage. I meet them at the pool hall every Friday night. After a few games of pool we head for the local drive-in, where we jump the fence and begin planning.

"Let's break into the bar tonight after hours," Roger says quietly. The three of us are huddled at the back, sipping beer that Roger's brother bought earlier.

"Nah," I say. I don't want to tell him that my parents expect me home by one o'clock at the latest, after the drive-in movie is over. I don't want to sound like a "pussy."

"What d'you want to do then?"

"How about that lumberyard behind the fence here?" I motion with my beer.

"Lumberyard!" Roger snorts. "What d'you think we'll find in a lumberyard? Nails?"

"There's probably some money in the till, because who'd think of breaking into a lumberyard?"

"You're probably right, Tyman. This one's yours. We'll wait for you here." Roger nods at Matt. Matt says yeah, it's my turn, and hurry up we're running out of beer.

Up until then I'd watched them with sweating palms and knocking knees as they raided a house, looking for valuables or something to drink. "Just ring the bell two or three times to make sure no one's home" was Matt's fearless advice. But now it's my turn ...

I scale the fence that surrounds the lumberyard. A dog barks. My heart stops. It's not a guard dog. I creep up to the office, ducking behind a stack of lumber every time a car passes by outside the fence. I come to a window. The till is right there! Now what? Beads of sweat are stinging my eyes as I peer around for a rock. I find one. Clasping it in my hand, I close my eyes. There's no turning back now. The sound of breaking glass fills the night. Even the dog stops barking. I turn to run, but I tell myself I have to do it. I race back and pull myself through the window. I cut my hands, rip my coat and pants. I fall to the floor in a crumpled heap. I jump to my feet, heart racing, face sweating. My hands are shaking as I dig into the cash box. There's no money! I can't believe it. I throw the paper over the floor: checks, money orders, receipts, bills, but no money. Finally I grab the tray from the cash register. It's full of change and a few rolls of dimes and quarters. I leave by the back door. I race to the back of the compound to count my take and get rid of the money tray. Damaging evidence. I bury it in a pile of gravel, a few inches under. I figure they'll find it and be happy they got it back, and they won't be so mad then. I slip under the fence to the drive-in. I make my way over to my two friends, who are happily drinking beer and talking.

"How much did you get, Tyman?" Matt asks.

"About $50." I speak sheepishly. "But it's all in change, quarters and dimes."

"Money is money."

It was my first break and enter, and the beginning of a crime wave in Fort Qu'Appelle. But I didn't do any more break and enters with those boys. Something told me not to trust them, and I knew the only way you get caught is either red-handed or from someone else talking. They knew I was up to something, but they usually forgot about it when I offered to buy the beer for the weekend.

Things got pretty hot in Fort Qu'Appelle. The newspapers published warnings about the recent rash of break and enters in the community, telling people to keep all valuables off business premises. The police had their turn in the papers, too: "There will be foot patrols in the community to help capture the suspect(s). We are currently following several leads. Any assistance in helping to stop the rash of break and enters will be appreciated."

I read the articles and I told myself, "Just one more, then I'll quit." But it never happened. It became a game of cops versus robber with the foot patrols. And many nights when all you could hear were the crickets chirping and the waves lapping on the beach in Valley Center Park, I'd be walking home with my pockets full of petty cash from the evening's work. I'd walk along the moonlit beach and look up at our house, which was visible from most points in town, and I'd wonder where my life would be now if I hadn't been adopted. Would I be stealing? Would I still feel sad most of the time? I wondered how many brothers and sisters I had. I wondered who the white one was.

* * *

My father was very cheerful Saturday mornings, after he and my mother came back from shopping. "Come on, son, get up and get something to eat." Mom always had bismarks and long-johns, or sometimes just plain sugar doughnuts for us. Dad would tickle my feet till I squirmed with laughter. "We'll do three loads before dinner," he'd say cheerfully. He meant three loads of cement in the wheel barrow. We were building a stone wall. I was the cement mixer and my father was the rock layer. He was proud of me then, for I was such a hard worker. He couldn't stop praising my capabilities to anyone who came up to see us. My brother-in-law, Al, was one of the ones who listened, and he called on me when it came time for baling hay. Then it was his turn to praise me, and soon job offers were always coming in for this 15 year old who worked as hard as a 30 year old man!

I was working hard all right, trying to show everyone that I wasn't like those "lazy Indians" who littered the town, drunk and crude, every time they got their welfare checks. I was a hard-working white man; that was what I was trying to prove to my family, my friends, and anyone else who saw me. I was fighting myself.

I usually had a hangover Saturday morning — dry mouth, dizzy vision, the whole works. If my father had his suspicions they were quickly banished by my tenacious work. We put in long hours, usually from 10 in the morning till 10 at night. There was always work to do. We built sidewalks around the house; we built wooden steps; we put the siding on. After the stone wall was finished we built a chimney for the fireplace. Between all these work projects we built a fence — my two brothers, Don and Bill, myself, and my father — around the eight acres that my father and oldest brother jointly owned. In the fenced-off area we had one mare at first, then she had a colt which became my horse.

Some days I'd spend hours riding that old mare through the hills and fields above the valley, and frequently through the streets of town. I enjoyed the moments when I was alone, riding the crest of the valley and looking down on the town. Fishing was one of my great pastimes, too. Hours and hours I'd spend on that same foot-bridge that I crossed after nights on the prowl with Roger and Matt.

To my family I was a hard-working, clean-cut youth. Then on weekends I was pulling three or four break and enters a night, just so I could buy friends and influence people with beer, drugs, and romping good times. Inevitably, my two lives crashed together. When the dust had settled, my roller-coaster emotional life had derailed. I had crossed the line. There was no turning back.

MAY 1979

It was a warm day. I was riding my bike around town sipping a beer through a straw; I had ingeniously poured it into a Coke cup to camouflage it from the police. I decided to head over to the Hanson house; I'd heard their parents were out of town for the weekend.

"How're you doing?" I said to Francis as I rode up their driveway.

"Not bad, chum. Whatcha drinking?" I showed him. "Jesus, Jimmy, you're always drinking beer." He smiled broadly. "Give me a sip." He took a big gulp. "God damn, that's warm! Come in the house, I got some cold stuff."

We sat in the basement drinking beer and shooting pool. Things were going well. After we'd had about six apiece, Francis' older brother William — the one who was on his father's side when it came to Indians — phoned the house. He wanted some change for the store their father ran in town. The boys all decided to go down to the store and deliver the rolls of change, just for something to do. I had different plans.

I told the boys I'd be going now, since my mom had planned a big supper, with guests coming. I left with them, then turned off toward home as they continued to the store. I waited till they disappeared around the corner, then doubled back to the house. It was unlocked, and there was a briefcase full of the weekend receipts inside. I was going to get back at that racist bastard.

I pulled to a stop casually in front of their house. I walked to the door and rang the bell. I waited a minute before pushing it open, then shut it casually behind me. Once inside I raced to their father's bedroom. I glanced under the bed. Bingo! I unsnapped the latches and opened the briefcase. There were five envelopes with elastic bands around them. I looked in one. I saw nothing but checks at first, but at the back of the bundle there were hundred-dollar bills! I couldn't believe it. I counted off seven right away. I'd been pulling petty break and enters with maybe a hundred-dollar take once in a while. But now I was looking at wads of cold, hard cash! Three of the bundles were nothing but money. The other two were a mixture of checks, gas receipts, the tape from the till, credit card receipts, and more money. With shaking hands I grabbed all five bundles. I tucked them into my pants and shirt, and as casually as possible walked out of the house.

I was feeling disoriented suddenly: I was going to go home, I was going to return and put the money back, I was going to go to a field and bury the treasure. Finally I decided to stash the money in the alley and head for the store. I knew there was going to be heat, and I wanted to make myself look clean.

"Hey Jimmy, I thought you were going home," Francis said in his naturally cheerful tone.

"Nah, I figure I got a half hour or so. I thought I'd come by, seeing your lovable father ain't here to run me off."

We both laughed, then William came up and told Francis that their father had called; he was giving him shit for leaving the house with all the money inside. Andrew and Phil raced home to check on the money while Francis and I stayed back. Francis was talking, but I wasn't listening. I was waiting for something else to happen.

"Francis!" It was William shouting from the door of the garage. "Someone just stole Dad's money!"

Francis' face lost expression. "What! ... How? ... When?"

"Andrew just called and told me! Get home and wait for the police! They'll be coming over right away!"

I rode back with Francis to their house. He was obviously distressed. Guilt started to well up inside me. I was going to take him to the money, tell him it was a joke I was pulling on his old man and William for being mean towards me. But it sounded so unbelievable to me, I knew he'd laugh in my face, if not punch me. I was silent.

We got to the house. Andrew was very nervous when he was explaining the situation. They were all fearful of their father's wrath when he found out what had happened. Things were pretty tense. They started yelling at each other.

"Hey, look guys, I got to go home," I said. "I'll call you later." I was feeling sick to my stomach. I hated myself. I went to the stash of money, tucked the bundles in my shirt, and headed for home. I stopped just before our driveway. There was a clump of bushes there, out of view of the house. I pushed my bike up into the bush. I took the bundles out and started to look more closely at their contents. There was almost $5000!

"What's wrong, Jim?," my older brother Bill asked as I stepped onto the balcony.

"Nothing, why?"

"You look a little pale." There was no fooling Bill. "Come on, Jim, I know something's wrong."

I went over and sat down. "The Hanson's house just got robbed and ... well, I was over there this afternoon, and their old man really doesn't like me at all. I know he's going to blame me. The cops will probably come looking for me."

Bill laughed lightly. "That Hanson probably robbed himself." He laughed a little more. "I'll tell you something, Jim. I have this police officer friend. One day we got to talking about you over coffee. He said you're one of the good kids in town. You hang around with some bad kids, but you're one of the good ones." He put his hand on my shoulder, comforting. "I wouldn't worry about it, Jim. The cops know you're a good kid. If they talk to you, just tell them what you know and that should be that. Here, have a sip, calm yourself." He handed me his rye and Coke. I gulped the whole thing.

* * *

I'm eating supper but I can't taste the food. My stomach feels like a live volcano getting ready to erupt. I fake smiles as my father tells one of our guests, my brother-in-law's father, what a hard worker I am. Al's father is saying how big and strong I am for my age. I cut his lawn on weekends. He's always talking sports. I glance out the living room window. I'm waiting for the police car. Supper is almost over. And here it comes, the blue and white RCMP cruiser! I feel sweat forming on my back. I go outside and wait for him, trying to look surprised. He looks serious.

"Hello, Jim. I'm Constable Dempsey. I think you've been expecting me."

"Not really. I think I know why you're here, though."

His expression has not changed. "You know the Hanson's house was robbed."

"Yeah."

"I'm going to have to ask you some questions."

"I didn't do it."

"I didn't say you did. But you knew there was money in the house, right?"

"I knew he kept some for the store, but I didn't know there was any there today."

"Weren't you there when they left to deliver some money?"

"Well, yeah. But I didn't go with them. I thought it was just change they wanted." My eyes are fixed on the floor of the cruiser.

"Is your father home, Jim?"

"Why?"

"I'm going to have to ask you and your father to come down to the police station so you can give us a statement of what you know about all this."

My head is bowed. "I didn't do it."

"There should be no problem, then. I'd like to talk to your father, though. Can you get him for me?"

"Yeah. Just a minute." I don't know why he needs my father there to ask me questions. I stop at the bottom of the stairs. I can hear him joking with his family and guests. I take a deep breath. I start to climb.

I stand stone-faced at the top of the stairs. I motion for my father to come over. I whisper to him, "Dad, there's a police officer downstairs who wants to talk to you."

My father looks surprised. "What for?"

I can't tell him. I turn and go down the stairs, motioning for him to follow.

"Hello, Mr Tyman. I'm Constable Dempsey. I'm investigating the robbery of a large sum of money from the premises of Mr Hanson. I understand that James was at the residence this afternoon" — the guy sounds totally different now that he's talking to my father — "so ... uh ... I need him to make a statement. Since he's only 15, it is required by law that a legal guardian or parent be present. Could I ask you to bring James down for a statement?"

"Yes, I see no problem." My father's face is as serious as Dempsey's. "But why is James under suspicion?"

"I want to make it clear that I'm not pointing the finger at James. I just need his knowledge of the events this afternoon."

My father nods and turns toward me. "Did you take Mr Hanson's money?"

I put on my best innocent face. "No."

Dempsey and my father stare at me. Finally my father breaks the silence. "What time do you want us?"

"About seven or eight o'clock."

"Fine. We'll be there." My father gives me a smile, then without a word he walks back upstairs to his guests and family. I stand there for a minute or two, looking at a point just above where Dempsey was standing, where the insulation is packed between two floor joists. I'd stuffed the money in there.

My father and I drive to the police station in deathly silence. I've made a commitment: I'm going to be so cool that Dempsey will have no choice but to let me go. My father finally breaks the silence as we pull up in front of the police station: "I believe you, son. We'll just get this cleared up and get the hell out of here."

I was feeling pretty confident when I walked into the interrogation room. I knew my father was on my side.

"Just have a seat right there, Mr Tyman, and Jim. I'll be right back."

We sat in silence. I kept hoping Dempsey would come back and tell us we could go home, the investigation is over and Jim had no part of it (adding his apologies to my father and me and then shaking our hands). Boy, was I dreaming.

"Okay, Jim." I watched him put down the date and time at the top of a lined sheet of paper. "Okay, Jim. Just tell me what time you got there, what you did while you were there, and what time you left." His face was fixed in stone.

I started to talk. Dempsey started to interrupt. He wanted details: Who was outside when I got there? Who was downstairs when I was playing pool? How many beers did we have? What type of beer was it? Were Francis and I the only ones drinking? Did I drink often? He was trying to throw me off balance, demanding so many details. And every time he asked a question he fixed a piercing glare right into my eyes. I answered him with coolness. I made a few jokes. He was like a statue.

"Okay, Jim. Let's talk about what you did when you left the Hanson residence." He wrote as he spoke.

"I was heading home, but then I decided to go and talk to Francis some more, so I went back to his house. When I realized there was no one home, I went to the store."

"Why did you go back to the house?"

"I thought Francis or Andrew might have come back, and I wouldn't have wasted a trip to the store."

"No, Jim." Dempsey stared hard at me. "Why did you go back in the first place?"

"Well, like I said earlier, we were drinking beer. I was feeling pretty good. I thought I'd have a few more."

Dempsey leaned back in his chair and sighed. His face looked human again. "Well, Mr Tyman, I believe Jim is innocent."

I blew it then. My father started talking about honest mistakes that anyone could make. I relaxed and broke into a grin — the same kind of grin a kid has when his mommy catches him with his hand in the cookie jar. Dempsey caught that sly grin. Our eyes locked. He knew, I knew, everybody but my father knew that the police had their man.

My father was still talking away when Dempsey interrupted him. "Excuse me, sir. Jim, just to clear the air, we'd like to give you a polygraph test."

"You can't do that," I blurted out.

"Yes, we can," Dempsey lied. He couldn't hook me up to a lie detector without my consent, but he had succeeded in showing my father that I was opposed to it.

"Is there something wrong with that, Jim?" my father asked.

"We'll also have to take your fingerprints, Jim, and check them with the ones we found upstairs, since you said you were never upstairs." Dempsey quoted my statement from the written sheet in front of him. I wasn't sure if he was bluffing.

"I might have been upstairs!" My voice got louder. "I can't remember!"

My father sensed something was wrong. "What do you mean, you can't remember? Did you or did you not go upstairs?"

"I might have. Yeah, I went to get a glass for the beer." My father nodded. I knew he was convinced, and it was tearing me up inside.

Dempsey turned up the heat a few degrees: "Jim, do you know anything about the B and Es that have been happening around town?"

"What's that got to do with me?" I tried to sound annoyed.

"Well, Jim, your name has been brought up a few times in connection with them." Dempsey spoke slowly. "I was just wondering why."

"I don't know. Some people don't like me. Probably the gang leader and his buddies told you this, right?"

"No." His face muscles didn't move.

"Well, I know nothing about them." I shrugged my shoulders, but he wasn't buying it any more.

"We got a fingerprint off one of the B and Es, Jim. As soon as you give me yours, we'll compare them."

I felt the color drain out of my face. I was caught and I knew it. Dempsey was just turning the screws harder. "What place is that?"

"The medical clinic."

It was over. I hadn't been wearing gloves that time. I remembered grabbing the glass to get it unstuck from my shirt. I played my last card: "Well, I was there. I saw the guy go in, and I ran up to yell at him to stop. But when I put my hand on the window I cut it. I pulled the piece of glass out of my hand. That must be the one you're talking about."

Again my father nodded his head. He would not believe these accusations against his hard-working son. "That was a stupid thing to do, son. But I can see why your prints were there. You should have just looked for a police car."

Dempsey wasn't phased at my father's support. "We found blood inside, Jim."

"He must have cut himself, too."

"Same blood type, Jim."

"So?"

"The fingerprints we found on the window were the same ones we found all over the office."

I bowed my head. I had no more cards to play. There was a long silence. My eyes began to water.

"I did it."

"What about the other ones, Jim?"

"It wasn't me."

"Don't make it any worse, Jim. You'll be 16 in three months. Come clean now or we'll charge you then, and you'll be treated as an adult. The juvenile courts are a lot more lenient than the adult courts." He softened his voice and expression. "We've had you under investigation for a while now, Jim. It was only a matter of time before we got you."

I looked at my father. He was still rattled by my first revelation. I said, "I'm the one the papers have been talking about."

Dempsey stood up and said he had to get more files. I turned away from my father. I couldn't look at him any more. His head was bowed. He was doing his best to maintain his composure, but it was too much for him. I had broken his heart. He sobbed lightly.

"I'll leave home for a while, Dad, if you want."

"No." He struggled to speak. "I am your father and I'll stand behind you through this."

I still couldn't look at him. "Thanks," I replied feebly.

Dempsey returned with a stack of files. He was obviously in a better mood than when he had first come up the driveway, a lifetime ago.

"First things first, Jim. Where's the money you took today?"

I still had a little pepper left in me. "I never did that one."

"Do you want us to get a search warrant for your father's house?"

Your father's house. I remembered the stacks of money in the insulation. At first I thought he'd never think of looking up there. But then I thought of the dogs sniffing about, and how good they were at finding stuff by scent, and I decided to give the entire match to Dempsey. "The money's at home. When do you want it?"

"I'll get it right after we're finished here." Dempsey began listing off the B and Es around town. I could sense my father dying a bit more every time I admitted to one. Dempsey saw it, too; he went as fast as he could. When it was over, 13 break and enters had been wiped off the books and I was to be formally charged with the two most serious ones: the Hanson's residence and the medical clinic. Come court time the other 11 would be brought up, but Dempsey said the judge would give me consideration because I had confessed and had cooperated with the police. It didn't make much sense to me, but I could tell he was glad that he was the one who caught the bandit of Fort Qu'Appelle, and not one of his comrades.

Dempsey said no one would know, even when I went to court. "No one will be present. The only people who will even know you're going in will be the ones going to adult court. They'll see you go in, but they won't know what for."

He seemed sure of himself when he told me that. But, like any bad news, it spread fast. I was embarrassed. All my work to show my white friends that I was a "good Indian" had gone wrong. All my inner turmoil to show myself that I wasn't like the rest of the Indian race who drank, fought, and went to jail had gone wrong. "You actually broke into all those places, Jim?" I'd look dumbfounded for a moment. How did they know? Someone was getting the word out! Even after it was all over, Dempsey was still coming up to the house and asking me if I'd done this or that. He said he was tying all the loose ends up. And every time, afterwards, I'd find my father standing at the living room window, staring down with a grave expression, and I'd have to explain what Dempsey wanted this time, and he would just stare at me in heartbroken silence, until I turned and walked away. Then I felt his eyes on my back as he wondered if his son was telling the truth or not. I hated Dempsey for bringing this unnecessary grief down on my father.

About the only ones who were pleased with the revelation of my guilt were my two Indian friends. "Let's pull a B and E at the grocery store. I bet they got a lot of money in the safe," Roger was speculating. "You must know how to break into safes, eh Jim?"

He obviously thought I was a skilled burglar. Why disappoint him? "Yeah, sure. But I'm already going up for 13. Why make it worse?"

His eyes widened. "Thirteen, yet! You got guts, Jim. But you'll only get probation."

"Just probation?"

"Oh, yeah. You won't be 16 for another three months. You're smiling all the way."

I wasn't smiling, but Roger had a grin from ear to ear.

I was convicted in June, with a stiff warning from the judge that if I was ever again before him for an offense of a similar nature, the full force of the judicial system would come down on top of me. He wasn't smiling when he said it. No one was smiling.

SEPTEMBER 1978

I started grade ten with new notoriety. If some of my schoolmates didn't know, they were sure to be filled in by the ones who did. The local vultures were always wanting to know the spicy details of each crime: How much money did you get? Did I know where to get a gun? Did I have a gun? It was ridiculous, but that's the way people act when they're gossiping: they all end up with their own version of the truth. Then I was getting blamed for things I never did.

"You broke into my uncle's garage, didn't you?"

"You stole my bike the year before last, didn't you?"

It was a small town with one high school, and there was no way to get away from these questions and accusations. I wanted to quit school, but I never had the guts to tell my parents for fear of causing them more heartache. My sisters and brothers graduated before me, some with high honors. I didn't want to shame the family any more by dropping out. To be a convicted criminal as well as a high school drop-out would really make me look like a typical Indian.

Floor hockey and football helped keep me in school. The coach laid down the law: anyone caught skipping school would have his sweater and his place in the locker room permanently removed. It worked during the football season, then there was floor hockey. Come spring, though, and I was off doing more important things, playing pool and pinball. I was getting away from "prison" for a while. Even so, I didn't skip out of school as much that year as I did in the next two. I skipped one class for a whole year and I passed! It was easy to figure out: the teacher didn't want me back. I was a bad influence. Only new teachers bothered to comment on my behavior any more.

My father and I engaged only in necessary conversation now, when we worked together or when we sat at the table. I was like a zombie. "He just stands there like a damn zombie!" he said one day after church, with a disgusted look on his face. I didn't say anything. I didn't care. I used to enjoy the atmosphere at church, the serenity and the peace. Now I hated to attend. To me it was full of spiteful, self-righteous hypocrites. Besides, my Indian friends were telling me this was honky stuff.

My father was quick to fly off the handle when I stepped out of line. He was unreasonable sometimes, but I know it was his pain that caused him to lash out at me. But that changed, also. We became more and more distant. A typically dismal report from school used to send him into a tirade; now he just shook his head and set it aside. I thought then that he'd given up on me, as my teachers had. As I did, eventually.

1980

I finish grade eleven feeling pretty good. I had a good year of football, and was considered for lineman of the year but a graduate got it instead. I really enjoy football because I'm good at it and it gets me to a lot of parties with the good kids of Fort Qu'Appelle. My image has been important to me this past year. I shun people the in crowd doesn't approve of. I'm trying to show everybody once again that I'm a "good Indian." I'm popular because of my football talents, not because I'm a good Indian, but I don't care. It's something.

My favorite hang-out is the new arcade in town. It's where all the good kids meet and plan their weekend parties. I'm there night and day; home is just a place where I get my basic needs looked after now. I can't wait to get out of there. I don't like working with my father any more. We usually end up fighting over some trivial matter. We're both acutely aware of the growing distance between us, but trying to narrow the gap just seems to widen it. One day, in the heat of the moment, he says, "Don't bother coming back!"

Fine! He doesn't want me any more, then I'm going to the States. I saddled up Fred, my horse, and rode 19 miles to a town called Indian Head. I rode in silence. I didn't talk to Fred the way I talked to that dog years ago. I thought telling your troubles to a horse was an insane thing to do. Actually, I never talked to anyone but myself about my problems. A lot of people tried to ask me what was wrong, but my tongue was tied. "Keep it inside and drink hard whisky" was my motto. I did drink a lot, and I encouraged others to drink, mostly on weekends with the boys from the football team. There were drugs around, and I used them once in a while, but the in crowd generally shunned them, so I did too.

I spent the day roaming around Indian Head and making plans. I'd been straight for over a year, but now the thought of stealing a car came to me. I decided instead to ride on to my sister's and brother-in-law's farm. It was another 15 miles! It was dusk by the time I saddled up Fred again. I rode west, following along and about 200 yards off the Trans Canada Highway. It would take me to a dusty little town called Qu'Appelle, nine miles away. Then it was six more miles to Donna and Al's.

Soon it was too dark to see where I was going. I knew there were train tracks running along to Qu'Appelle, so I headed for them. After about a mile following the tracks I spotted a house lit up, with people drinking outside. They couldn't see me because the night was so black. Then I found myself riding across a railway bridge. Fred panicked when his hooves started slipping through the ties. I tried to pull him back, but that only added to his confusion. He fell through. If a train came now he was dead meat.

The boys I'd seen drinking at the house told me excitedly that there was a train coming in 10 minutes. I demanded help. They were pretty drunk, but I felt confident: they were wearing cowboy hats and this was a horse in trouble. With a few ropes and a push from below, Fred was saved from a very nasty death. He was carefully led off the bridge. By this time the boys were wondering where I came from, but a young lad came running up to say that Sue had phoned the police. I was already on the horse, so I gave a quick jerk on the reins and we lurched off into the darkness.

"Just answer a few questions!," they shouted after me.

"Stay for a beer, at least!"

I didn't know if my father had called the police, but I wasn't going to stay and find out. I saw the car lights coming down in front of me, so I turned off the road. I must have got 20 yards in when a branch caught me in the chest and pulled me right back over Fred's rump. The night was pitch black, but I found Fred again. The car passed. Soon I could hear the cowboys interrupting each other to talk to the officer. After 10 minutes the police cruiser hadn't come back, so I guessed my father hadn't phoned the cops. I decided to walk Fred back to the road. One fall was enough.

I was on the last leg of my journey—just another six or seven miles of total blackness. A person who jumps at strange noises in the night should never do what I was doing. You hear rustling in the bushes. You hear "something" scampering in front of you. You hear "something else" passing behind you. You don't look, for fear of seeing something, but you know that if you could only see there'd be nothing to fear ... probably. Fred wasn't phased at all. His ears would prick up at a noise, but then they'd relax. He was tired. So was I.

I found the back gate of Al's farm on the second try, and I got Fred into the barn just in time. The wind was picking up and it was apparent that a storm was coming. I filled a pail with water and placed it in front of Fred to drink. Then I went to the other side of the barn, where I used to throw bales of hay. It was as good a place as any — dry and comfortable, despite the scurrying barn mice. I wondered if some rat was going to chew my nose off if I fell asleep. I closed my eyes.

I awoke to find my body parts intact, and the voices of my father and brother-in-law outside the door. I heard Al say I wasn't here. I heard my father insisting that he open the barn door. It opened.

I didn't say a word. I could see my father's pain. I wanted to feel something, too, but there was nothing. I felt guilty only when I discovered that the water I'd given Fred was full of grease. "Poor guy hadn't had a drink all night," I told myself.

But I didn't feel that way when my father told me how he drove the fields all night looking for me.

1981

My father and I had planned to build one more rock wall together, but the plan keeps getting put off. He hasn't seemed himself lately. He drinks Maalox like water, says his ulcer is hurting. Then he comes home to tell us he's going to Plains Hospital in Regina. It seems like a routine thing: he's going to get his ulcer cut out and that will be that. He seems nervous when he asks me to get him some reading material from the drugstore, but I figure there's nothing to worry about.

It's a typical January day, cold and grim, when I see Donna and Al coming up the driveway. I turn down the stereo; I don't think they'll appreciate AC/DC at ear-splitting volume. My sister comes up the stairs with some books. "Jim, why don't you sit down for a bit? We have to have a talk." The look on her face tells the story. My father has cancer.

"When will he come home?" She doesn't answer. "How bad is it?" She shakes her head. "Will he live?" She wants to answer, but it won't come out. I am numb. This can't happen. She tells me to pack a few things. I'll be staying at the farm for a while. We'll be going to Regina tomorrow. This isn't happening. He'll recover. My old man is one tough cookie.

I lie awake at night wondering what could have happened. I remember all the good times we had together. The bad times make me shudder with shame, wondering if I'm the reason for this. I know ulcers are caused by stress, and God knows I've put him through a lot of stress the past couple of years. I wonder if that's a contributing factor. Of course it is! I toss and turn. I can't sleep. I want to scream. I really do love you, Dad! Please recover! I'll be good from now on! I'll make you proud of me please Dad hear me don't die! I won't cry. I'll just lie here praying to a God I long ago lost faith in.

We arrive at the hospital and my mother is smiling. Things can't be that bad, then. She tells me he's doing fine and he's glad we're coming to see him. Most of the family is here. I talk to my father. He seems so healthy. He keeps sneaking puffs on his pipe and laughing at the nurses' angry warnings. He's the most cheerful person in the room. He asks me how school is going. "Fine." He asks me how his dog is doing. "Fine." I tell him he'd better get better, we've still got that rock wall to finish. He says he will, and even if he's still sick he'll be kicking my ass to keep up with him.

They discovered the cancer when they did the operation for his ulcer. The doctor cut out what he could, and my father was given chemotherapy to help slow it down. They say the recovery rate for this type of stomach cancer is only 40%. I don't want to believe it, but it becomes apparent in subsequent visits to my father that we're not going to finish that rock wall. I feel helpless. I hate the visits to the hospital. Each time my father is in more pain. He's losing weight. The nurses have taken his pipe away for good.

I drink long and hard. My friends wonder what's wrong. Usually I'm a loud drunk, always telling jokes. Now I sit like a mortician. I lose it temporarily one night at the outdoor rink where we've been drinking. I start smashing the lights, chucking beer bottles at parked cars, screaming. My friends are worried that I've finally flipped my lid. Francis comes out of the warm-up shack when he hears the glass smashing.

"What's wrong, Jim?"

I look wild-eyed at him. I can see his worried expression turn fearful. He is good people, I tell myself. He's still my friend, despite the robbery I pulled on his father two years ago. I start to relax. I whisper to him, "My dad, my old man is going to die."

"Ah shit, Jimmy. I'm sorry, man." He is truly sorry. "But don't start smashing things. Someone'll phone the cops on you. You don't need that kind of shit, man." He offers me a sip of his beer. "Come back in and take it easy for a while."

Francis, what a good old shit he was that night. I needed comfort and he did his best. I didn't tell anyone else. I put up a front for everyone.

* * *

I'm walking to a nearby mall from my sister Margaret's house in Regina. The day is so cold you can see ice crystals in the air. I hate being here. Last week I told my family I didn't want to be here any more. Watching my father wilt away was too much to bear. I felt guilty and helpless. So I was sent home. Now I'm back in Regina, at my mother's request. My father's condition is very grave. At my last visit he was barely conscious. He took my hand and kissed it. He whispered something I couldn't understand. I fought the tears. I had to leave the room. "There's no God," I told myself. My father who had been so strong is now a human skeleton. He is given shots of morphine to dull his agony. I keep hoping for a miracle, something the doctor overlooked, some new wonder drug.

I return to my sister's house. I go into the basement, where I've been sleeping for the past couple of days. I lie down. I wonder when it will be official. What a horrible feeling, waiting for someone to tell me. I know it's imminent. I close my eyes and drift off to sleep.

"Jim, Jim." It's my sister. Tears are streaming down her faces. "Mom called, Jim." She stifles a sob. "Dad died 10 minutes ago." She breaks down. I stare into space. I should cry, but there are no tears. Now that it's happened I feel nothing. Just like a zombie. I get up and look out the window. Everything seems normal, as before. People driving by in cars, the wind still blowing, the snow still white. Nothing's changed. Life goes on.

The house is filling up. Tears are flowing, family members hugging each other. "It was a mixed blessing," Donna comments, my eldest sister. "Now he won't have to live in such pain any more. It's a mixed blessing," she says to anyone, to everyone. It's a blessing of some kind, that's for sure. He was in so much pain, his body had deteriorated so much. I couldn't stand to see him like that. He was such a proud man. But I feel awful. He died when we were in such turmoil. He was my guide, my inspiration, my teacher, my father. I don't care if I was adopted, he was truly my father. And this is wrong. We weren't finished. I'm only 17! I want a father. First they took me away from one, and now I've lost another.

Things were quiet those first few weeks after it happened. I was silent in school, didn't cause the teachers any of my usual problems. Then one night when I was out with the boys I snapped. I climbed onto the roofs of buildings along Main Street, hauling full garbage cans up with me so I could throw them back down. Soon the street was littered with debris. My buddies knew I'd snapped. They stayed inside the local pizza joint, peering out the window as garbage cans flew through the darkness. Then I went after the pizza man's fence. It was only three feet wide and seven feet high, blocking off the narrow passageway between two buildings. I kicked it apart and threw the boards onto the street. I was about to put a match to a pile of garbage when my faithful friend Francis grabbed me by the arms and led me to his car.

"Jesus, Jimmy, you're going to get into trouble for this." He was lecturing me and laughing at the same time. "You're getting crazy again."

I knew he cared, but it didn't matter to me any more. "I'm just having fun!"

The investigation wasn't a long, drawn-out affair. Some of my schoolmates had seen me doing it and they couldn't wait to tell the police. I was sitting in Francis' car when the RCMP cruiser rolled to a stop beside us.

"Hey Jim. Get a little upset there?" I didn't answer him. "I want you to come down to the station for a bit."

It was quick and formal. I admitted my guilt and he handed me a promise to appear — a paper that had the charge written on it (mischief) and the date and time I was to appear in court.

At my first appearance I had the date set over till summer. I'd be finished school then and I figured it would be easier to break the news to my mother. She was so kind to me. But somehow I knew I was going to break her heart, as I had broken my father's.

* * *

I won the trophy for top lineman on our football club. It was all I was striving for that year. The rest of the year was just putting in time, sitting at the back of the class, sometimes drunk, talking out loud, hoping the teacher wanted to fight. Suspensions were looming over my head all the time. One day eight of us were called in to see the vice principal. He was determined to clean up the school, and we were the ones he was going to crack down on. He had a list of our offenses: throwing chalk at students and teachers, knocking books out of each other's hands in crowded hallways, stealing lunches, using foul language. He ended his half- hour speech with a promise: "These acts will stop, or you guys can look at a little holiday from school."

We did cool it for a while. Then one day when six of us were supposed to go for school pictures we went to the liquor store instead. We picked up 48 beer and two bottles of Cherry Jack, and off to the country we went. After two hours of steady drinking we made a brilliant decision to return to school. One guy dropped the bottle of beer he had under his coat just as the vice principal came out of his class. There was foam all over the floor and no need for an explanation. The vice principal simply pointed and shouted at him to get off the premises. Meanwhile, two other guys had grabbed the human skeleton from the biology lab. They were about to hang him from a tree in front of the school when the vice principal, with the principal in tow, came through the doors. They chucked the bones back in the carrying case and ran with it through the parking lot. Finally they just dropped it and jumped into a car and sped away. I jumped in Francis' car and we sped off, too, laying John Doe to rest in the high school parking lot.

Three hours later I was driving my late father's car down Main Street when I was waved to a stop by one of my accomplices.

"Hey dude! Whatcha doing?" I had consumed a bottle of wine and was working on a few brews.

"Jim, we got suspended!"

"How do you know?"

"Look here." He showed me a letter. "It was in our mail box. My mom or my dad has to come talk to the principal on Monday."

"They didn't waste any time." I started to read the letter.

"You're not kidding."

"It was the vice principal. He wanted to hang us out to dry, remember?"

"You shouldn't have got us to go drinking."

I laughed at him. "Don't start blaming me for your inclinations."

"Yeah, well, it's your fault," Kent said.

My mother was not going to be pleased about this at all. She had shown such strength in the past few months. At my father's request she was selling our house and moving back into town. I was peeved at the idea, but I never told her. I thought we were selling out on him. But that was my heart thinking, not my head. We had our own well, which needed to be cleaned regularly. We had our own sewage system, which needed regular maintenance. My mother didn't have a driver's license, so getting around would be hard; I was the only one left at home and I wasn't going to be there forever to drive her around. I could see my father's logic. Still, it hurt to have to sell his dream house.

The house we eventually moved to was convenient, though: across the street from the police station. When I was released in the mornings I would just cross the street to my other home. The troubles for my mother were just beginning. But that evening I just spent trying to come up with a reasonable explanation for my suspension from school. In the end I just told my mother it was all in fun, and that no harm was intended. That wasn't the point to her, but it was the only explanation I could think of, and it wasn't a complete lie.

On Monday morning we drove to school together. The principal's hands were shaking as he explained the details to my mother: suspension from all school activities for the remainder of the year. These suspensions didn't mean anything to us, though; they were a message the vice principal was sending to the younger students. We were graduating the next month. Three weeks later I was out of there for good.

I received my high school diploma from a smiling principal, with the school auditorium full of my family and the townspeople snapping photographs. There was only one problem: I knew I didn't have the required credits. I guess they just hoped I'd be happy with my certificate and say nothing and, more important, never come back. I didn't tell anyone, but the feeling in my gut was that this was wrong. I wasn't supposed to graduate. The proof came in my final report card. I'd failed every subject.

"You're up early," my mother said as she watched me pulling on my sneakers. "What for?"

I'd left it to the last possible moment to tell her: "I'm going to court."

"Oh no, Jim. What for?"

"Just mischief." I sounded nonchalant. "I'll get probation probably, maybe a fine."

"What did you do?" Her face looked worried.

"I kicked a fence down." I walked to the door. "I've got to go."

I received a $50 fine, $25 restitution to the owner of the pizza shop, and six months' probation. When I stole thousands of dollars in cash, check's, and money orders along with 12 other break and enters along the way, I received three and a half months probation. Now, for doing less than $25 damage, I received my first criminal conviction as an adult. I was officially marked for life, for nails and paint.

* * *

I'd been "free" for two weeks when I landed a job as a meat-cutter and clerk at a local grocery store. Two weeks into that job I went on another spree. I'd made friends with a high school dropout and a kid who just couldn't meet the standards of the in crowd for some reason: Warren Rollins and Terry Harvey. Rollins was small, 150 pounds, with Beverly Hills blond hair. Harvey was two inches shorter than me, but with a smooth, almost feminine complexion. The three of us hung around that summer, and it looked as though I was making some friends. They were white, which helped my image with the towns-people. That was important. We made a strange trio, though. The only thing we had in common was the fact that we didn't have fathers. But the friendship taught me a valuable lesson: never trust a fellow thief.

Our crimes were bizarre and senseless. One night we broke into an old public school. It had been shut down long ago, and was now rented out for community-oriented classes. I watched in disbelief as Warren started tipping over the seven-foot mirrors in the room used by the ballet class.

"Jesus, Warren! Why're you doing that?" Terry demanded.

"Because they're here!" He let out a roar as another mirror shattered in a loud crash of glass. I cringed. This was not the thing to be doing on a burglary, making all this senseless noise. I couldn't quite understand why I was there in the first place. I guess I just hadn't wanted to seem like a sissy. Terry was obviously a thief—I watched him going through desk drawers and filing cabinets — but Warren was just destroying. And whatever was running through his mind when he was breaking those mirrors was still there when we went to the local drive-in about two hours later. As Terry was trying to knock the hinges off the door to the concession we again heard the unmistakable sound of smashing glass. I knew there was a huge window up there; it used to be for people who didn't have cars, so they could still come in and see the movie. There was room for about 20 people. It took Warren a dozen throws of a large rock to make a big enough hole for him to get through.

"I tell you, Terry" — I was shaking my head — "that guy is going to get us busted."

"He's just a little hyper, that's all."

I couldn't figure out why Terry would defend Warren. The pair of them came to blows almost every weekend. They had a strange relationship. This was a strange crime.

When we got inside Warren was busy smashing everything in sight. He tried to steal the film projector, but it was fastened securely to the table, so in frustration he ripped up all the film he could find. Terry started looking for the cash box and cigarettes. I watched them in silence. Finally it hit me that this was my chance to blow off steam. I started chucking things around — chocolate bars, chips, anything I could find. Warren was besides himself with enjoyment.

"Right on, Tyman! Wooohhh!" he hooted, tipping over a soft drink fountain.

I tipped over the other fountain, then I shouted, "Let's get going! There's nothing in here!"

Warren agreed. We drove up and down Main Street for about an hour after that. Terry had his mother's little Honda Civic. Warren had decided to steal two gigantic bags of popcorn before we left, and he sat squashed between them in the back seat. We were seen by at least a dozen people who later asked us what the hell those huge white things were in the back seat.

Warren and Terry decided to go to Regina then. They tried to convince me to come with them, but I had to go to work in three hours. It was a good thing. They were about 15 miles outside the city when Terry fell asleep at the wheel. The car was headed for the ditch when he was jolted from his sleep by a shouting Warren, who grabbed the wheel and pulled the emergency brake. It was too late. The car flipped over. It skidded along the asphalt on its roof, then rolled several times before coming to a halt on its side. The pair emerged unscathed, with popcorn blowing in the morning breeze.

It was Mrs Harvey's new car. Fourteen hours ago Terry had told her he was going to use it for an hour or so. Since then it had been used as a getaway car in two burglaries, and now it smelled of popcorn and beer, and it looked as flat as a pancake. Terry was not amused.

* * *

It was September 29th, 1981, and I was out celebrating my 18th birthday with Terry. It wasn't until the next day, actually, but I thought I'd get a head start. Terry had finally had enough of Warren, and would no longer talk to him. We were driving down Main Street when Terry spotted Warren in the car in front. Warren spotted Terry, too, and gave him the finger. That infuriated Terry. He gave chase. It didn't last long. Warren's car pulled to a halt right in front of the police station. Warren jumped out and ran in. Our hearts sank. It wasn't much later that three police cars cornered us and we were placed under arrest.

There was a local cop we called "Bigfoot." He was always pulling people over and giving them tickets for minor infractions. He'd smile broadly as he leaned his massive head through your window to tell you, "If you don't pay this ticket, I'll come looking for you." If he enjoyed giving out tickets so much, he was in seventh heaven when he had me in his office. Bigfoot and Mr Hanson were pretty close friends.

"Well, Tyman." His face was beaming. He sucked in his gut and pulled his pants over the bulge. "You've been busy this past summer. Rollins tells me you and Harvey have been pulling break and enters all over the place. I'm going to put a stop to that right now!" He put on his best menacing face. "Do you want me to help you? Or do you want me to hurt you? I helped Rollins, now I can help you. What d'you say, Tyman?"

I don't know why I didn't just admit my involvement. Rollins had given Bigfoot details about the B and Es. He told him what we'd been drinking. He told him who had bought us the beer. He told him how much gas Terry had bought for the car. He told him how I was the one who'd wrecked the fountain machines at the drive-in. One other thing was becoming apparent as Bigfoot talked: Rollins was innocent. Rollins was just following us. We pushed booze down his throat. We influenced him to use drugs. Now he wanted police protection.

I stretched my hands out in disbelief. "I don't know what you're talking about."

"All right, if that's the way you want it." Bigfoot opened the door. "Take this guy and lock him up."

I sat alone in the cell, wondering if Terry was going to talk, too. "What a week," I whispered to myself. First, I had no job any more — the store got sold to one of my old teachers, and I was let go because I didn't fit into his plans — and now this.

Fifteen minutes later Terry was escorted back to the next cell. "Fuckin' Rollins!" He sounded venomous. "That low-down, good-for-nothing, stinking rat! You know what he's been telling Bigfoot? That I've been selling drugs in school! What a bunch of bullshit."

"I take it you didn't say anything?"

"Rollins said it all for me." He paused briefly, then glared at me. "And you?"

"It looks like we're going to get made. No use fighting it. We'll get probation ... I hope."

"Sure, it's our first offense." He sensed something in my tone. "It is your first offense, isn't it?"

"No. I've got a juvenile record for the same shit."

"Oh. I can see why you said 'I hope'." He started to laugh, but he could see my displeasure. "Come on, Jim. You won't go to jail."

"What makes you so sure?"

"You were adopted, for one thing. And you were adopted by

a white family, for another. You've got a great sob story for the judge." He started laughing again.

I was speechless, then I asked, "Why would that make any difference?"

"Because you'll be pitied. You had a rough childhood. But now you're with white people, so things must be looking up. That's what the judge will think, and he won't want to break it up by sending you to jail with a bunch of rank Indians."

I stared hard at him. I was angry. I wanted to speak out, but I couldn't find the words. I turned away and lay on the bunk, wondering if what he said was true.

Morning came with the rattling of keys. The guard was a man who used to tell me jokes when I went to visit his sons. He didn't bother looking at me. He didn't utter a word. He just shoved our breakfasts under the cell doors and walked back out. I could see his contempt. I could feel it. I didn't care any more.

"Happy birthday, Jim." Terry smiled.

"Fuck you!"

"Whoa! What's the matter? Wake up on the wrong side of the bed?" He was still smiling, but he was startled at my reaction.

"We're cooked," I said. Then I shouted out, laughing: "I'll confess! I'm guilty! Take me away!"

"Shee-it, guy. You seem different. You had a nightmare or something?"

"I'm free! The world is great!" I rattled the cell door. "Wooohhh!"

"Settle down in there!" the commissionaire shouted.

"Your mama!" I shouted back.

Terry sat in stunned silence.

"I demand a phone call! I demand to see a lawyer! I know my rights!" I let out a roar of laughter, then sat down to my eggs and bacon.

"What's all the shouting about?" a local cop asked gently.

"When're we getting out?"

"That's up to the officer. He'll be in at ten. You can ask him then."

"He'll want us to write a statement. We're cooked anyway.

Hey, let's go to the beach and have a party tonight!"

Terry was still a little mystified, but he was always up for a party. "Well, it is your birthday." He smiled devilishly. "What about picking up some smoke? Get high, too."

"Why not! Make a day of it." I roared with laughter. Terry joined me this time.

Bigfoot came and was visibly surprised when we agreed to write a statement against ourselves. He couldn't get us out of the cells quickly enough. I signed a confession to three break and enters, damages over $2000. I didn't care. I just wanted to party, have fun, pick fights, and experiment with drugs.

Everyone in town knew about my latest escapade within a week. There was no way in the world I was going to get a job in this town. My mother knew it, too. She was busy looking in the Regina paper for me.

"Why?" she would ask me. "Why? Didn't we give you everything?"

I wanted to tell her that that wasn't the problem. I got everything I needed, except a sense of identity. I knew that this she could not provide. I just didn't know who I was, or where I came from. No one told me. No one seemed to care.

The party lasted a month. Then my mother found me a job 90 miles away in Moose Jaw, as a meat cutter in a grocery store. I knew it would help my sentencing in court. My mother was hoping it was the thing to settle me down. She bought me a car for the occasion.

Some friends of hers had found a room for me, just off River Street. I could sense my mother's excitement as we drove to Moose Jaw to check it out. But the room and the building were obviously below my mother's standards. It was a rooming house, actually. The landlady was a barmaid, and all her tenants were in the lower income bracket. I couldn't figure out why my mother wanted me to take it so badly. I was just glad that she was glad. I guess she was relieved that I wouldn't be living at home any more. She paid my first month's rent.

Moose Jaw is a small city, with a population of around

45,000. River Street is Moose Jaw's version of "the strip." The street itself was a mile long, but all the action took place in one three-block area. I was conveniently placed one block away.

I started my new job in early November. The work was familiar, and I blended in well with the daily routine. I cruised Moose Jaw at night. On my first two-day break I went back to Fort Qu'Appelle to see my old buddy Terry. He was starting to get more heavily into drugs, and so was I.

It was raining lightly, and turning to ice on the road. On the way home, at about 20 miles an hour, I slid off the road and into a cement post which raked the side of the car from the wheel to the door. The car was totaled. The police officer who came to investigate decided I'd been driving without due care and attention and gave me a court date. I'd had the car for six days.

With my mother's backing I went to the bank and obtained a loan for $1500 and bought a Dodge Duster. The engine had been modified for racing. Nights back in Fort Qu'Appelle I'd be roaring down the same road that my first car got wrecked on. The speed limit was only 25 to 40 miles per hour. I'd usually be going 80. The thought of crashing didn't bother me at all. I wanted to crash sometimes. I wanted to go up in a ball of flames. I wanted to die in glory. I drove with one hand on the wheel and one hand on a 40 ounce bottle of Canadian Club.

When I wasn't driving I'd be sitting in one of Moose Jaw's downtown bars — drinking, watching, and learning. There were people there who were obviously into criminal activity. They'd be walking from table to table, having huddled conversations with people. Sometimes they were carrying shopping bags, and while they whispered they'd open the bag up slightly and someone would peek inside. I watched in fascination. I didn't know then what they were doing, but drug trafficking was very common in these bars. I noticed a lot of individuals were carrying knives strapped to their belts. At first I thought they were hunters or fishermen. In time I found out the knives were used for sticking people on the street, not for skinning game or boning fish. It was strictly lethal protection.

A lot of Indians drank there, and a lot of white people. Back in Fort Qu'Appelle you just didn't see this — whites and Indians sharing beers and, obviously, poverty. I guess poverty breaks down those invisible barriers, and wealth strengthens them. But they had some kind of respect that I couldn't understand. If they'd been living in Fort Qu'Appelle, I thought, they'd be frequent occupants of the pool hall, and shunned by the community. Here people were always coming up to talk to them and buy them beers. The bartender was taking their calls, the waitress was delivering their messages. They were important. They were mostly of Indian ancestry and they were obviously criminals. But they had respect and fear, and apparently a lot of friends. I could sense it was wrong, but I wanted it. I wanted people to respect me the same way. I wanted people to come up to me and shake my hand and buy me beers. I wanted it, and I was going to get it.

I was to see a probation officer in Moose Jaw. I didn't tell him about my white family or the fact that I was adopted. I didn't want to believe what Terry had told me in jail that morning. But when my probation officer went to see Cecile, my third eldest sister, he was obviously taken aback. She could see his confusion, and finally she told him that I was adopted.

"Oh well," he said. "That changes quite a few things."

My sister asked what difference it made. He didn't answer, but shook his head and began to make notes on his writing pad. I felt terrible when my sister told me this. "I guess Terry was right. I got a sob story." I hated pity. I was going to get respect and fear, not pity and scorn.

* * *

I was shunning Terry occasionally, and he knew it. I was dividing my time between Moose Jaw and Fort Qu'Appelle, work days and weekends. Back in fort Qu'Appelle the in crowd wanted nothing to do with Terry since his arrest with me for the break and enters, and now the rumor of his involvement with drugs. It was strange. I was just as guilty, but I wasn't completely shunned. At least they talked to me. They ignored him altogether. But I wasn't to be accepted, either, so I kept going back to the "undesirables" of Fort Qu'Appelle. There was plenty of marijuana to go around, lots of booze, and discussions of violence were as common as the in crowd's discussions of sports. They were two radically different groups of people: one used drugs very seldom, while the other used them like cigarettes and bubble gum. One group talked about careers and soap operas, while the other talked about crime and far-out sex. I would listen intently. "These guys would fit right into those bars in Moose Jaw," I told myself. But in Fort Qu'Appelle they got blacklisted.

1982

I arrived at the court house for sentencing about ten-thirty; my appearance was set for eleven. I was bored. I knew now that I was going to get probation. Rollins and Harvey had each received two years' probation with curfews, reporting to a probation officer, and abstaining from alcohol. The last two conditions worried me. Terry had already busted his probation three times for breaking curfew and boozing. If I got the same conditions I knew I'd be the next to be charged with breach of probation. Abiding by an eleven o'clock curfew for two years seemed unconstitutional, and to have to abstain from alcohol for the same amount of time—never. I liked drinking. I enjoyed sitting down and sharing a cold beer with my friends. It was something I looked forward to every weekend. It was my chance to be a part of something. But I had nothing to worry about. It was all over in five minutes. There was no curfew, no alcohol restrictions. I just had to report to my probation officer, and to make restitution in the amount of $750. I never did pay.

Now I was on probation for two years and my outlook on life was distorted. I had no identity. My experiences with the court system just added fuel to my anger. I felt like a token at work

— somebody who was needed to fill a place for what he is instead of what he knows. My mother had made it a point to come and see my boss when I applied for the job. She just wanted to show him that I came from a white family and that I was a good Indian. I wanted to quit. But I had a bank loan to pay off. I was tempted to sell drugs for Carl, an Indian I met in the Brunswick Hotel on River Street. I was feeling pretty good from the booze when I started to tell him about my so-called friends in Fort Qu'Appelle, and how they were looking for drug deals, and that I was well known down there and I could sell lots of drugs for him. He hemmed and hawed for a minute. He asked if I'd be willing to sell drugs in Moose Jaw first. I was reluctant. I told him I didn't know anyone in this town, but I'd give it serious consideration. He smiled and said I was "good people." I smiled back and said, "You mean, a good Indian." He looked bewildered, and I felt stupid. He must have thought I was bonkers or something, the way he looked at me. But I thought everyone knew what a good Indian was: it's an Indian who has white friends.

Later, Carl would tell me that honkies don't care about Indians: "They pretend they do, but what it boils down to is this: if you stay on welfare, stay on the reserve, or stay in poverty in the city, then you'll be treated better. But as soon as you start making noise about being discriminated against, they'll turn it back in your face. They'll call you the bigot. They'll say you're not appreciative of what whitey is doing for us."

Carl was always talking about the money to be made living off the streets. "Working? You should be selling drugs and running whores, Jim. With your size you'd do good in the downtown scene."

I tried to sound nonchalant. "Well, if I get fired or quit or something, I'm sure I'll hit the streets."

"Great, you'll find there's more money and freedom on the street than you'll ever find in any nine-to-five job with a bunch of honkies. To hell with them, Jim. You don't want to be a token all your life, do you?"

I stared at him for a long, silent minute. Was this guy living with me or something? How did he know how I felt?

"No, I don't want to be a token all my life."

I wasn't going to be a token, I swore to myself daily. Some nights I'd go to the bar and pick fights. Bartenders would phone the police, but I always slipped away before they came. It calmed me for a while. I started to count the days when I could quit and collect unemployment insurance; that way I could at least pay off my car. I had thoughts of pulling a few jobs in Moose Jaw, but I wasn't ready. I didn't have the nerve yet.

I walked the mall in Moose Jaw, always aware of the floorwalkers following me. I studied people. Could it be true, what Carl said? Us versus them? Why? Why can't we work together? It's so tragic. I have good white friends in the Hanson boys, but their father hates me. I walk by a group of Indian girls. They smile at me. I blush. I can't believe this, either. The Indians in Fort Qu'Appelle seemed to hate me more than some of the white people did. They said I was an apple — red on the outside, white on the inside. I guess the Indian girls in Moose Jaw didn't know that. I never did stop and talk to them, though. I was an Indian, but I felt uncomfortable with them unless I was drunk.

My buddies back in Fort Qu'Appelle were noticing my changing behavior. They thought I was just drinking too much, that's why I was talking about honkies all the time. I confronted them with what I'd learned, about what the white people did over the past hundred years. I recited cases that I'd heard about on the radio or seen on TV, about Indians taking the government to court over some land rights violation the government of a hundred years ago had committed.

"Damn, Jim, I wasn't here a hundred years ago!"

"Yeah, but remember what you said about how the Indians are getting too much from the government already. Shit, man! Look how much the white people took in the first place. And they're still screwing them. They tell the world they understand the Indians' dilemma, but they won't do anything to change it."

"We understand, Jim. But the Indians shouldn't take the government to court. Look what the government does for them already."

It was like taking one step forward and two steps back. And I was getting uncomfortable around white people — all white people: my family, my few white friends, my probation officer. He was part Indian, but I assumed he was just an apple. That's what all the Indians said when I asked them about him.

In March of that year I was walking around River Street, stopping to talk with a few of the people who had grown accustomed to seeing me there. They were always happy and talkative. They'd tell me about the trip they went on last night, or the wild party that lasted for three days. They'd talk about going to Regina to party it up for a while. I'd smile and nod my head, but it was amazing to an 18-year-old small-town bumpkin to see these people flash money around and talk about going places at the drop of a hat, or party for three days without any obligations. They scoffed at work, honkies, and authority. More important, they had respect. They had identity. They were street people. That was their identity, their worth, and they loved it and accepted it. I wanted it. I quit my job within a week.

I didn't hit the street, though. I went back home to Fort Qu'Appelle. Whatever security I'd ever had was there. I'd learned a lot in those few months in Moose Jaw, but I wasn't ready for the life I saw there. I wanted the street image but my conscience was still out, like a jury. I was awaiting its decision, good or evil. I told my mother and my friends that I was fired because the boss's brother had made a pass at me and I knocked him down a flight of stairs, breaking his arm. I didn't want to tell them the truth. I didn't want them to think I was a typical Indian who couldn't hold down a job.

I got my nose broken that month. I was fighting with a farm boy over a girl. I made the mistake of turning away, and he caught me with a right cross to the temple. It knocked me unconscious for a moment, but I woke up when he jumped on top of me and continued his assault. By the time I was dragged to my feet and thrown in the back of a car I was in pretty bad shape. I had to stay in bed for two days with a concussion. It was the first and worst beating I ever took, and I swore revenge if it ever happened again. Of course it did, right after my nose had healed.

We were partying up at a buddy's place. His parents had just built a new house in the hills about four miles outside Fort Qu'Appelle. It was the Easter long weekend, and five of us had holed up there. His mom and dad were in Arizona and weren't due back for another week. I was in possession of about $300 worth of vodka, whisky, rum, and gin. I was in a party mood and this was a great opportunity to kick up my heels. I had never drunk so much in my life as I did on that day, and ever since then I've never consumed that much alcohol and still been able to walk. I had woken up about six that morning to see a local girl drinking straight whisky out of my bottle. Rachael was 15 years old. I was still drunk and took a long swallow myself. She was giggling. When I asked her why, she pointed behind me. Her panties were on the lamp shade. She pointed to another lamp, giggling louder. Her brassiere was on top of that one. She laughed some more and passed out. I shook my head and walked away.

By six o'clock that evening I had drunk two 40s of whisky and was working on a 40 of rum. A local halfbreed named Tom came in and we started to party with him. He was only 19, but he already had false teeth. I knew it was time to rest when I'd nearly finished the rum. I was lying down when Tom came barging into the room, shaking me and demanding that I give him back his teeth. I made a few choice comments and he left. Then I heard him in a loud voice tell everybody how I'd stolen his teeth, and how I was probably going to give them to my biological mother when I found her. That did it. I stormed out and grabbed him by the arms and threw him against the wall.

"I never stole your fuckin' teeth! And watch what you say

about my mother!"

"You had them!" he shot back.

I was ready for a fight. I knew the guy was left-handed, so I was waiting for his left hand. He hit me with his right. I saw it coming, but my reflexes were too slow from the booze. He caught me on the nose. I heard the unmistakable cracking sound, and suddenly there was blood pumping over the walls, my shirt, the furniture. I went to the bathroom and, squeezing my nose between my palms, I moved it back as best I could. I'm glad I was full of pain-killer. I grabbed a bottle and was about to smash his head with it when everyone started yelling at me to stop. I was steaming, but I was too drunk and too damn mad to fight. I went back to the bathroom to check on my nose, and that's when Tom slipped out. I gave chase. I had a bat in my car and an extra tire iron for just such occasions. But the guy must have read my mind, because he pulled the wiring out of my distributor cap. Now he was safe, and probably so was I. I'd have been sure to go to jail if I'd done what I wanted to do to him.

My nose had been busted before, but now it was obvious. It was bent to the right. Once again I swore that if anyone should come close to harming me, I'd fight back with a passion. I was boiling with fury. I wanted violence. I needed it.

I was partying lots with a few diehard buddies. One of them was a guy whose passion was drugs. It was his house we'd been partying in at Easter, and it was his girlfriend who'd shown me her undergarments hanging over the lamps. Another was the farm boy who had busted my nose the first time. We still found companionship with each other, maybe because his father was dead, too. On a typical night we'd cruise around in my car, smoking dope and drinking beer. We used the side streets because my car was just too well known and the local police were out to nail me — for anything.

It was about eleven-thirty one night when we decided to call it quits. I was about a mile from home when I saw three police cars dead ahead, about three blocks away. "Shit!" I swore. "I'll try to deek them out." I turned down an alley and drove through someone's yard onto the next street. The police cars were moving. One was coming down the alley that I'd just driven off. The others were closing in from different directions. I thought my quick maneuver might have got me past them, but when one of them swerved directly in front of me I had no choice but to stop. Within seconds the other two cop cars came to a screeching halt with their red lights flashing. The households nearby drew back their drapes, or opened their front doors. I imagined the telephones already relaying the news through the community.

The farm boy was busy stuffing marijuana down his shorts. The one joint we'd been passing around Rachael stuffed in her bra. The roach was only an inch long. We knew they were going to frisk us, but they couldn't touch the girl.

The pungent smell of marijuana rolled out of the car like fog when a cop pulled open my door. "Jesus Christ!" he exclaimed. "All right, everyone out of the car! Jim, open this trunk!"

I watched as two police officers started to search the interior of my car, looking for grass. They found nothing but empty beer bottles, and a couple of half-full ones. "That's good for one ticket," I told my dumbfounded friends.

A cop motioned for the farm boy to follow him. He told him to drop his pants. How embarrassing. There were five cops there, and onlookers on their front porches, some others peering nervously through their curtains. My friend complied, and the cop was visibly upset at not finding any contraband. I thought we were home free. The cops were standing around, talking among themselves. They weren't going to ask me to drop my pants. One of them handed me my ticket for the open liquor in the car, and with ice in his voice told me to go home. I was about to do as I was told when a rookie cop told everyone to hold it. He called Rachael into my car. He put her in the back seat, while he sat in the front. I don't know what he said to her, but my heart sank when she reached into her shirt and pulled out the one-inch joint.

"Throw these two into the back of the car." He spoke loudly, holding the roach high for everyone to see. I told the farm boy to say nothing. I said, "We had no drugs on us. What can they charge us with?"

We sat in jail overnight, exchanging guesses about why we were being held. My friend hid the remaining marijuana in the cell. He hid it so well that 13 months later, when I was in overnight, I smoked a joint!

It was about ten o'clock the next morning when a cop came for my friend. Two minutes later another came and got me.

"Well, Jim." He was stone-faced. "I've got some good news and some bad news."

I smiled cheerfully. "What's the good news?"

"You're going to get out today." I didn't change my expression. "The bad news is this: you're going to be charged with two counts of trafficking cannabis resin, and two counts of contributing to the delinquency of a minor, plus two counts of breaching your probation. Your liquor ticket has been upgraded to a court decision, since it's the second time this month you've been caught with open liquor in your vehicle. Your car has been impounded, and you'll have to pay the tow bill before you can get it out. It comes to $25. You also have a flat tire. You'll have to get that fixed before you take it out. Any questions?"

"Yeah. You got a strong rope?"

"No, I don't." He wasn't laughing. "I suggest you get a lawyer, Jim. These are serious charges. The contributing to delinquency carries a minimum of a year in jail, and the trafficking carries a possible life sentence."

I was sitting in the cells when the farm boy came in, white as a ghost. The charges had shaken him.

"Don't worry. We'll beat these trumped-up charges. Rachael won't testify, she was just intimidated. I wonder what he said to her," I pondered out loud.

"She said that I was the one who had the drugs, and that I was the one who'd influenced everyone to smoke pot." His voice was cracking. "She said she just wanted a few beers, and the pot was my idea."

Later, I walked down the street to the post office to see if my unemployment check had come. I needed tow fees now, and a boost because the police hadn't bothered shutting off my headlights. I also had to have a portable air pump brought down to blow up my tire, which had a mysterious slow leak after that.

I was almost there when out walked my mother. "I hope you're proud of yourself! It's all over town, what you did!" Her face spat hatred. "Here." She handed me my unemployment check. I turned away without saying a word. I had broken her heart completely.

* * *

I met Ricky walking around town while my car's front end was getting overhauled. I'd often seen him standing on Main Street, listening to his ghetto blaster. He was rumored to be a little psychotic, and slow in the head. He told me he was epileptic: "I take medication, so if I seem a little dense, don't make fun of me. I'm not retarded. The medication makes me that way." He looked at me with soft blue eyes. He was six years older than I was, and 220 pounds of solid muscle. I wasn't about to make fun of him.

I tried to sound calm. "What type of pills are you taking?"

"Phenobarbs." He flashed a grin full of yellow, chipped teeth. "You take lots of them and you get real screwed up."

I'd heard about people taking pills in town; they were the ones who were usually trying to commit suicide. They'd be rushed to the hospital to have their stomachs pumped out. "Let me try some."

He gave me six white tablets. I downed them in one swallow, then waited, and waited.

"Are you getting high yet?"

"Not really. I feel kind of drowsy."

"That's what phenobarbs do. Just fight the urge to sleep and you'll be right high." He gave me another winning smile.

"Give me some more," I demanded.

"I need them, Jim. I might have a seizure. Then what?"

"I'll jump on your chest, or whatever you need. Now come on, give me some more!"

He snorted. "You don't jump on my chest. Just make sure I don't swallow my tongue."

He handed me six more tablets. Within 30 minutes my balance was erratic. I was staggering, and slurring my words. We decided to grab some beer and go to a party in Lebret. By the time we got there I'd convinced him to give me 20 more phenobarbs. I only drank four beers all night, but I was falling all over the place. People were laughing. I got back home at seven o'clock in the morning. My bedroom was downstairs. I fell the last six steps. I was out in a flash.

I woke up about three in the afternoon, still drugged. It took me 10 minutes to climb the stairs. I walked outside and headed for the arcade. It took 30 minutes to walk four blocks. I staggered to the back booth where Ricky was sitting.

"You look like you're still screwed up, Jim."

"Give me some more," I said. "I've got a headache and those things will calm me, right?"

He grinned. He knew what I was up to. "Sure, Jim. But I got no more left. You ate 30, 35 last night!"

"Well, go get some more. You must have a prescription or something!" I sounded like I'd been hooked for years.

"I got no money," he said sheepishly.

"I got some. Let's go." I got up on wobbling legs and motioned for him to follow me.

"You've had enough of those things, Jim. Look at you! You're still staggering from last night!"

"I'm just tired," I told him, "and I sprained my ankle. Quit being a nursemaid and get your prescription."

Ten minutes later he had them, but I never asked for any until seven o'clock. I was weaving pretty good till then, and as long as I knew where they were I was happy. I was severely out of it by ten o'clock. I had to lean against cars, buildings, anything to help me with my balance. I thought of going to the hospital. Then the police came. My behavior hadn't gone unnoticed.

"Let's go, Jim." It was the cop who was laying the trafficking charges against me.

"What for?"

He didn't bother answering. He and his partner each grabbed an arm, and off I went to the familiar cells.

"I demand a breathalyzer! I'm not drunk!"

"Didn't say you were!"

It was obvious I was going to spend the night in jail whether I was drunk or not. When I emptied my pockets I pulled out over 40 phenobarbs.

"What's this?"

"It's my buddy's medication. I don't know what they are."

"We'll have to send them to Regina to get analyzed." He was dead certain he had a bust. I laughed.

When they let me out in the morning I was in worse shape than when I came in. I kept falling backwards when I tried to put my shoes on. I was expecting someone to whisk me back into the cells. But they just told me the pills would be returned to their rightful owner after they'd been checked in Regina, and opened the back door for me to stumble out. It was a Sunday morning and I knew I would have to wait for another hour, so my mother wouldn't see me in such bad shape. By that time she would have gone to church, and I could slip into the house for a change of clothing and be off again.

It was only four months since I'd refused to go to church any more. My mother was aghast. But I couldn't stand to sit there and watch all the phonies singing their hymns and praying good will to all men, and two hours later asking me where they could find some grass. There were a lot of people in the community who had shown me prejudice, and here they sat in fine clothes singing the Gospel. To me church was a showpiece: "Hey look at me I'm going to church, I'm a good person." I didn't want any part of it. In all fairness, there were a lot of good Christians there, but just like in the rest of my life, the bad side influenced my decision to quit.

I spent the first few hours sleeping in the field behind our school. I awoke around one o'clock that afternoon. I was still in bad shape. I'd walk for 10 feet, then collapse, and every time I collapsed it took me a minute or two to get my bearings and stand up again. I made it to Main Street, where I saw my Indian friend Matt about two blocks away. I fell three times before I reached him. Why I wasn't arrested again is beyond me. I drifted in and out of sleep most of the afternoon, on the front steps of a business downtown. Matt kept a look-out for the police. When he finally shook me awake it was half past four. "Come on, Jim. Let's go down to Gene's for a coffee."

It was only a block to Gene's Kentucky Fried Chicken, but once again I found myself acting like some dazed boxer who keeps getting clobbered to the mat, and when we got there my head kept falling to the table.

"You're in bad shape, pal."

I grumbled something and went unconscious. Matt shook me awake again. He was telling me to come walk with him around town so the pills would wear off.

It was dusk before I finally felt better. At least I could walk down the street without falling off the sidewalk. I went home and straight downstairs. It had been four days since I last talked to my mother. I was asleep within a minute.

My farm friend and I had our preliminary hearing date in three weeks, and I had an appointment with my lawyer. He assured me they couldn't get a conviction on any of the charges, and his services would cost me $1000. I'd paid him a couple of hundred already and he was on my case for the rest.

"I'll pay you a couple hundred more come court time."

"Okay, Jim, but you've got to clear your account."

"Yeah, yeah. Now what about these charges?"

"I've been discussing it with your friend's lawyer and we feel there's a good chance of a plea bargain with the crown."

"I see." I tried to sound competent. "Like what?"

"Plead guilty to the lesser charge of possession, and they drop the remaining charges, except for the breach of probation and the liquor violation." He studied me for a moment. "You are guilty of possession, Jim."

"Does that mean fines, then?"

"We'll have to see. But this isn't final about the plea bargain. I'll be in contact by phone to let you know the final decision."

"I'll be waiting for your call," I said, and as I got up and started for the door, he called after me, "Don't forget the money, Jim." I nodded and closed the door behind me.

I spent the three weeks partying with Ricky and Matt. There were no more phenobarbs for me. My futile attempt to overdose had led to a severe state of nausea for three days, and even after that I still didn't feel quite right.

"Are you on pills or something?" My mother had her familiar, worried expression.

"No, no. I'm just feeling sick. Stomach flu, I guess."

She nodded. I wondered if she was catching some of the gossip. I felt like a celebrity: if I had a legal problem, everyone knew about it; if I had family problems, everyone knew about it. People love dirty laundry.

One night I had six people over for a party. Six people shouldn't be too hard to control, I thought. Within two hours we were all drunk and turning the stereo up to 10. The music was deafening. Our conversation and laughter was louder. My older sister Donna came over in the middle of a beer-guzzling contest. She was upset with me. I offered her a beer, but that just made her madder. After she was gone we decided to play football with the beer bottles. Terry would pin them and I'd try to boot them through the open window in the door. There were only three of us left: Terry, Matt, and myself. The act continued for about 20 minutes, then we decided we were hungry. I should have realized how crazy we were getting when Terry and

I had a game of knife fighting in the kitchen. We only stopped after I'd jabbed him hard enough with a butter knife to break the skin.

We ate most of the food in the fridge. Then Matt suggested he go over to his sister's, since she lived only a block away, and grab some more food. Terry decided to go with him, since he liked Matt's sister. While they were trekking to her house I decided to go next door to get an album I'd lent to my neighbor. I was informed by his very irate mother, who was not the least bit impressed with my banging on the back door at a quarter to midnight, that he was sleeping.

"You go home!" She slammed the door in my face.

"Hey, wait a minute." I started to bang on the window. "I just want my album. C'mon, you old bag! Open this ..." The window smashed to pieces. "Shit!"

"Go home!" She was shaking with anger.

"I just wanted my album." I turned and walked back to my place. I wasn't there five minutes when the front of the house was illuminated by the flashing lights of police cars.

"Who phoned you guys?" I demanded.

"Your loving sister." Bigfoot was smiling like an angler with a 10-pound jackfish.

I was thrown into the drunk tank this time. It had no beds, not even a bench. It was just a cement room with two fluorescent bulbs behind quarter-inch plexiglass. They were on night and day. There was a drainage hole for you to puke, or urinate in. I'd been cursing and hollering for 20 minutes when I saw Terry and Matt go by.

"What did you guys do?"

"Nothing!" Matt shouted. "We were in the house wondering where you were when Bigfoot came barging in with his friends!"

"Hey, Terry. You get charged?"

"Yeah, breach again." He sounded wounded.

I knew he was going to jail again. He got 30 days last breach of probation, and now he was sure to get more. I was wondering what my charge was going to be.

Morning came and I was moved to the more comfortable jail cells. "When am I getting out?"

"You're not!" the escorting officer snapped. "You're going to Regina. You'll come back for a bail hearing on Monday. Then it'll be up to the judge to decide if you're getting out."

"What the hell did you do last night to get all them cops to come over?" Terry was disgusted with me. He was blaming me for his arrest.

"I broke old lady Rogers's window. It was an accident. But I'm going up for those other charges, so I bet that's why they're going to make me pay bail money to get out."

"You shouldn't get bail. You're a bad influence. You have a bad attitude, and you're a rowdy, rank, motherfuckin' Indian who's selling drugs to school kids. That's how the cops will portray you in court."

"I see." I paused to study his expression. "I'm not a sad story any more?"

Terry was silent. He turned away to brood about his upcoming incarceration in Regina's infamous correctional center. It was called "The Hill" by old timers. I was headed there with him.

I had been informed that I was to be charged with mischief on the Rogers's window and breach of probation. I was sure I was going to get time finally. The bail hearing was set for Monday morning at nine-thirty.

The police van came, and off we went to Regina. We saw no one as we left town — no one to wave to, no one to remember. We arrived at the correctional center about four in the afternoon. Terry didn't talk at all. I wasn't scared of jail. It was more a kind of horrible wonderment. Do they really fuck each other in the ass in here? What type of person would do that? I wonder what a killer looks like? I wonder if there have been any murders in here lately?

We sat in the admitting and discharge area for about 15 minutes before anyone paid us any attention. Then the keeper shouted, "You two come here." We did. "Just go with this gentleman." He paused to glance at Terry, then grinned. "I think you know where to go."

We went through one barred door, then waited while the steel door in front of us buzzed and the lock opened to let us pass. To the left was a doorway that led into the shower room. We were told to strip, one by one, and enter the shower. After that we were issued clothes that didn't fit. We went through another steel door. When we got through that one there was one more. We came to the area called Basement Square. The smell of sweat, dirty clothes, and urine stung my nostrils. "Jesus it stinks in here," I whispered to Terry.

"The weight room is right there." He pointed to a doorway.

"We go to the gym?"

"Remand inmates go twice a day."

"Hold it." The guard stopped us and pointed to me. "Take him to West G." As I walked away I could see Terry smiling.

West G in the Regina Correctional Center is where they lock you up 24 hours a day. "Those cops in Fort Qu'Appelle must have done this," I told myself as the guard locked me in. The mattress had urine stains on one side, so I flipped it over. There were more stains on the other side, but at least it was dry. The cell was filthy. There were human feces smeared on the walls and the toilet seat. The stench of urine was overwhelming. Some lost souls had scraped their names on the walls. I started to read some; they went back 10 years. "Time to paint this cell again," I told myself.

I was eating supper when the guards brought a scruffy-looking guy about five ten and weighing in at maybe a 150. He was my cell mate. We wouldn't have given each other a second glance on the street, but when two people are locked in a nine-by-six cell, breaking the ice is the easy part; getting the other guy to shut up so you can go to sleep is the hard part. He talked of far-away places like Toronto, Montreal, New York City, Los Angeles. He was a gypsy by his own admission, and he couldn't wait to finish this sentence so he could head to Vancouver and down the coast to LA. After an hour of talk I found out his name was Allen Irving.

"It's beautiful to be able to travel around without any worries, except for the pigs!" He flashed a set of teeth that long ago died. "Shit, man, in the States they pull you over with shotguns pointing at your head." His laughter was a mixture of gurgles and deep breathing. "So whatcha in for?"

"Mischief and breach of probation."

"First time inside?"

"Yeah."

"I've been in seven times. Three in the States."

"How many times in here?"

"Three. No, this is my fourth time." He took a drag off his smoke. "This place is the dirtiest, that's for sure."

"How old are you, anyway?"

"Thirty-one. You?"

"Eighteen." I tried to sound older.

"Shit man!" He snorted. "When I was 18, I was doing two years already up in One F."

"One F is a range, I take it."

"Yeah. It's got only a catwalk — you know, about two and a half feet wide — in front of the cells. There's about 35 guys up there, all double-bunked, poor fuckers! Same size cells," he said, glancing around. "If you wanna watch TV you gotta go downstairs 'cause there's no TV up on One F. A lot of guys won't go downstairs. Bunch of pussies really. If you gotta beef, handle it. Don't run from it." He was lecturing me. "Take me, for instance. If I was as big as you are, shit, man, I'd be running things in here. Like, no one would fuck with me. Yeah!" He took an excited drag on his cigarette.

"You have problems in here before?"

"Me! No way, pal! No one's dared to fuck me around. Shit, man, if anyone did I'd kill him, or shank him. I don't take shit from anyone!"

I studied my little superman. His eyes were large with excitement. I was fascinated by his violent spirit. I'd never met anyone who talked like he did. I was tempted to ask him what the scars on his wrist and forearms were from. I had an idea, but I remained silent. I was still a nervous virgin in prison life.

I was there only for the weekend, but the days were long and monotonous. I did learn a trick at doing time in West G, though: throw butter or honey on the floor at night, so you won't have insects crawling all over you. There were six black and white televisions set up down the range. We had one right in front of us. I spent all Saturday lying on my bunk watching sports programs. I was already getting tired of being cooped up with Allen, the commando. He talked and talked, about himself or things he'd done, about the shortcomings of society: "If I was Prime Minister, I'd fire all the police and run the country with my own army. I'd get us outta debt, and we'd have the most weapons in the world. Even the States would be scared of us."

Monday morning I was pacing nervously while Allen dreamed of some mercenary mission in Central America. I was glad that at least I'd be getting away from this GI Joe. The guard came and I was hauled off to admitting and discharge.

The ride back to Fort Qu'Appelle was in silence. On the highway we passed the judge who was going to preside at my bail hearing. I was wondering if they were going to put me back in solitary if I didn't get bail. I had one chance: the judge was reputedly soft hearted, so if I laid a thick sob story on him I might get out. But I wasn't going to bend my knees for any court system! I decided to shut my mouth. Going back to Regina so I could have a shower was all I was thinking of when I walked into court.

I sat handcuffed with a police officer on either side of me. I had watched other men sitting like this. I thought they were murderers, or criminal masterminds. I felt stupid getting all this attention for a $24 window.

My eye caught the Indian court worker across the room. She'd glance at me and look at her file, then she'd shoot another quick glance at me. After a few minutes of this, she walked over and asked the two police officers if she could have a word with me in private. They nodded and got up, taking up positions where they could still keep an eye on me.

"My name is Evelyn Dumont, Jim. I'm a court worker. Have you contacted anyone for your bail hearing?"

"No."

"You don't have a lawyer?"

"Yeah, I got one. But when I phoned him Friday he was already out of his office so I decided to hell with it."

She looked dismayed. "You should have a lawyer for your hearing."

"If you're applying, you're hired."

"Well, okay then. Tell me, Jim, do you care if you get out?"

"Of course I do."

"I see. It's just your attitude toward the situation. You don't seem too concerned."

"I am concerned. But tears won't help, only money."

"You've got money or can get money for bail?"

"No. My mother might put up the money." I was hoping.

"Do you want me to give her a call?"

I thought about it a moment, then I gave her the number. What did I have to lose? I watched her walk to the pay phone. I was wondering what my mother would say about these latest developments. She had phoned me when I was being admitted into Regina. She was upset and hurting. I didn't want to talk to her when she was singing the blues, so I told her I had to go. I had no room for softies any more. Jail was just another inconvenience in my life. Or so I told myself. Maybe being tough was the only way I could face what was happening to me, and that meant being tough with everybody.

"Good news, Jim. She says she'll be over in 20 minutes with your brother."

It was almost court time when I saw them strolling in. Both of them looked sick at heart. My mother wouldn't look at me, but Bill shot an occasional glance in my direction. I felt like shouting out, "If you don't want to be here, then get the hell out!" I bit my tongue so I wouldn't start.

The police were adamantly opposed to my release, no matter

what the bail. Miss Dumont told the judge that I was only 18 years old, the support I had from my family, the fact that these new charges had no relation to the other, upcoming charges, and the fact that my mother had already paid Mrs Rogers the $20 for a new window. Then came the shocking discovery: Mrs Rogers hadn't phoned the police. Neither had Donna. It was the cop who lived next door to the Rogers — he'd phoned his buddies and charged me for breaking the window and breaching the peace. What a hero.

"Stand up, Mr Tyman." I stood. "I will give you a chance to stay out till you clear up these matters before the court. Bail will be set at $1000 property and $1000 cash. You are not to consume any alcohol or be in possession of alcoholic beverages, and you are not to have any contact with the Rogers family until you have dealt with this matter."

I waited in the back of the police station as my mother signed affidavits for my release. I learned from the escorting cop that Roger was trying for bail in Indian Head, because this judge had sentenced him before, and he thought the prosecutor might be less prejudiced against him in another town. It didn't work. He was denied bail. He pleaded guilty to the charge of breach of probation, and received four months in the Regina Correctional Center. He only came back to Fort Qu'Appelle periodically after his release.

* * *

I was in a sullen mood the night before my next court appearance. I didn't think I was going to jail, but I didn't really care. I had a premonition that jail was coming ... some time. My lawyer told me I'd walk in and receive fines and walk out, and to make sure to bring him his money. I was spending some of his money on booze and marijuana. "If I go to jail," I said, "he ain't getting another dime."

Court time came and I went drifting in under the calming influence of marijuana. I walked right into Rachael. She looked nervous. "I'm not going to testify, Jim. Don't worry." I nodded and continued into the court room. I wasn't supposed to make contact with her; it was one of the conditions of my release four months ago. I was sure it would be good for a charge if I were to stop and talk to her.

I spotted my lawyer. He was all smiles. "Things look good, Jim. Plead out to possession and you'll get a fine, plus fines for your two breaches and your mischief charge, and the trafficking counts and contributing to juvenile delinquency will be dropped."

"How much in fines?"

"I'll keep them low."

I sat in the third row watching the preparations. The cops were assembling their evidence: the half-full bottles of beer they'd got from my car, and the one-inch joint in a plastic bag. It was over in two minutes. All I did was stand up and acknowledge that I was James Tyman. I received two $75 fines for the breaches of probation, a $100 fine for open liquor in my vehicle, a $150 fine for the one-inch joint, a $75 fine for the Rogers's window, plus restitution of $25 and, to seal the sentence, 18 more months of probation. The other charges were dismissed.

"Jim, you've got my fee?"

I handed him $150.

"I thought you'd have it all today."

"I'll send you the rest," I said. But I never did.

The arresting officer met me at the door. "You got lucky, Jim. Next time ..." He turned and walked away.

Three weeks later he was smiling broadly as I was led into the police station with three more criminal charges against me.

It happened in Lebret. I was partying with a group of local Indians — with my growing notoriety they were accepting me more then ever — when I decided to take this guy's car. His name was Kevin. He was the cousin of a local Indian nicknamed "Mucky." Kevin was wanted for armed robbery and assault in Winnipeg. I didn't like him much. I found him to be a loud, obnoxious, self-centered asshole. So when I got tired of the party I decided to take his car. I knew from watching him when he drove me to the party that all you needed to start the car was a screwdriver and a twist of the wrist.

The people at the party came out to hoot and holler as I burned doughnuts and fishtailed around the house. I decided to head to Fort Qu'Appelle. I got about 100 yards when I lost control and swerved into the ditch. Mucky came up in his own car and told me to jump in, we'd go for a toke. While I was off with Mucky, Kevin phoned the police and reported his car stolen. Now the police were tripping over themselves, each trying to be the one to arrest me. They raided all the local parties looking for me, including one 10 miles out of town; Mucky had given them a bum steer while I was in a gas station using the facilities.

I spent the next day up in the hills with a few guys from a neighboring town who seemed to enjoy my stories of crime and illicit drugs. At dusk I was handing 24 beer to an under-age school kid, the son of the local pharmacist. I was to follow him and he was going to give me a few for pulling the beer at the local bar. The kid was trying to impress everyone by doing 60 miles an hour along the lake road. Francis and I decided to do the speed limit because we didn't want to spill the beer we were drinking at the time. About two miles outside town we rounded a particularly sharp corner to find the hero's car — or I should say his father's car — on its side, blocking both lanes of traffic. There were a few cops standing around, but they didn't pay much attention to me. I was walking away from the scene when one cop came running to place me under arrest. They had called in my presence and were just waiting for an escort to take me back, but my leaving made them break from their other duties. Back at the police station they presented me with the charges: taking a vehicle without the owner's consent, breach of probation, and impaired driving.

"Impaired driving? How the hell can you charge me with impaired driving?"

"We've got witnesses who saw you staggering about, drinking in public, and then jumping in the car and driving off. They've already been subpoenaed, Jim."

"You bastards! You went through all that trouble just for a charge?"

"You broke the law, Jim, and my job is to enforce the law. You sign this promise to appear and you can go." He handed me the promise to appear, the usual information: keep the peace, be of good behavior, stay away from Kevin, appear in court in two weeks to answer the charges.

I walked out knowing one thing: I was going to jail. I glanced across the street to my mother's house. I didn't belong there, either. This town was no good for me any more. Where could I go? I walked on. It was dark and there was hardly any traffic. I reached into my pocket and pulled out a joint. (The police hadn't bothered frisking me.) I smoked it as I walked. I decided to move to the city when I got out of jail. "Who knows, I might get rich," I told myself. I used to have dreams of getting rich, just to show everyone that I wasn't a typical Indian, content to stay in the shadows and collect welfare when he realizes white society doesn't want him. I wasn't going to let them do that to me. I would make them want me. I would make them notice me, and respect me. They would know who I was. But now it all seemed worthless. I was going to jail. I was just another typical Indian.

I had a new drinking spot then — an apartment behind a clothing store off Main Street. It was rented by a guy who had quit school long ago. He was considered a low-life scoundrel, even though he worked full time and was never in trouble with the law. But the in crowd delivered the verdict years ago and it stuck.

I might as well have moved in with Dale. Even when he was at work he left the keys with me or with Ricky, my constant companion. When he returned from work there would be a party in full swing.

I became friendly with a young girl we called Wicked Wanda.

She was officially blacklisted by the in crowd because she'd been caught stealing from the till in the liquor store. Then she was found with over $500 worth of stolen clothes tucked into garbage bags under her bed, and more over at her grandmother's house. She was charged with 15 counts of theft under $200, and one of theft over $200 for the liquor store. She was still waiting for a court appearance when I met her. She was 17 at the time. I had turned 19. She was a mix of Italian, German, and French. After a few weeks of steady partying we got into our first brush with the law.

Wanda had been suspended from school for various reasons, mostly for not being there. But she wanted to attend the school dance, so after putting away a 40 ounce bottle of vodka we showed up at the front doors. We found our path blocked by teachers and chaperons. I pushed a few people and challenged them to come outside to settle our differences. Meanwhile, Wanda had started arguing with the school principal. Then she started slapping his head. I was lucky enough to have a few friends present who whispered to me that the cops were on their way. I was pulling Wanda out the door when the familiar red flashing lights pulled up. My luck held, though, because the cop who took charge of the situation wasn't immediately filled with animosity when he discovered it was Jimmy Tyman he was dealing with. I had him convinced that it had just been a bad mistake to come here and that we were leaving, when Wanda suddenly gave him a left cross to the temple. Within seconds she had both arms pinned behind her and she was being dragged, kicking and cursing, into the back of the police car.

I watched open-mouthed, not believing that this pretty young girl could take swings at both a school principal and a police officer in the space of five minutes. She was whisked off to jail, but a police van stayed behind in the parking lot. I spotted a friend sitting in his car with a few other people, so I walked over and banged on the window. That was all the provocation the cop in the van needed. I had banged the window in an aggressive manner. I was under arrest for being drunk and disorderly.

When we got into the back of the police station I could hear Wanda screaming and hollering and threatening anyone who passed in front of her cell. I was required to lean against a desk while they frisked me down, then I had to empty my pockets. My heart sank when I took out a piece of tin foil folded into a tiny square.

"What's that?" the cop demanded.

I leaned close, as if to study it. "I think it's tin foil." I made a grab for it, but I was too late. I was quickly subdued by two uniformed officers. The cop behind the desk unfolded the foil and found two tablets of purple micro-dot acid. His face shone. He had his bust.

They let me out the next morning because they wanted to find out where I was getting LSD. Up until then marijuana and hashish had been the common drugs in Fort Qu'Appelle. Now they'd found acid, and I was the link to it. Two weeks later a local cop pulled me over and informed me that the charges would disappear if I revealed my source. I was appalled. No way was I going to pull a Judas.

"Fine," he said. "You're also guilty of breach of probation. When you go to court next week we'll have that charge waiting for you." And they did.

I drank hard. Everyone around me drank hard. The party never ended. When people drink hard, their emotions take over. My epileptic friend wanted to talk to me about suicide one day. He picked the wrong guy if he wanted compassion and understanding. I had as much of that as the cops did.

"Here, take this knife and slit your wrists!" I threw the knife at him. "Well, come on! Slit your wrists! I dare you! You've got no guts. You're a loser!" I stormed out of the room, slamming the door. I really did expect him to do it, but five minutes later he came out, asking me for a beer.

Then one night Dale slit his wrists and both his forearms with the broken neck of a 40 ounce bottle of whisky. He was about to start on his legs when I finally wrestled it away from him. I was pissed off because he'd smashed my 40 and not his. He grumbled his apologies on the way to the hospital. He said he'd get me another tomorrow. I told him to forget it. I'd get another right away. I had half a dozen stashed at a secret associate's house. No one knew who he was, but everyone knew I was up to something. I was a thief and he was my fence. I always had money.

* * *

My court date was set for just after Christmas, which was only six weeks away. If I was headed for jail and out of this town, I wanted revenge. I went on a crime spree with a couple of local boys from the reservation. They had connections in Regina where they sold our hot stuff, and they were the ones who had introduced me to Doug, my secret associate. That's how our relationship worked: I wouldn't give him a second glance if I passed him on the street. Doug wanted it that way. "You're such a heat bag, Jim. The cops are always on your ass. I can't afford that kind of attention, so come around late at night or phone me, but never let anyone know who I am. My image, Jim. My image."

He laughed when he said, "My image, Jim. My image." His image, all right; he had a lot to lose, being the respectable small businessman he was. I never had anything to lose, then or before. I'd been black-listed long ago.

I stayed at Dale's apartment for days on end, going home only for a change of clothes and a shower. I'd spend the days drinking with anybody who could keep up. Every second day we'd haul out 30 cases of empty beer bottles, and a box of assorted empties of vodka, whisky, rum, and wine. Between gulps of alcohol, I'd inhale marijuana or hashish smoke. I spent one week tripping out on acid. One night I took six hits, and pulled a burglary that I didn't remember till Wanda told me about it the next day.

The night before Christmas Eve I decided to spend the next day with my mom, since I'd been home only periodically since September. I watched as the police van drove slowly by. I didn't think they were going to start hassling me now. I kept walking. I was one door from home when the van swung around in the street and lurched over the curb, red lights flashing. It came to a halt in front of our house. Without any explanation I was grabbed and thrown in the back. The trek to the police station was short. The officer simply backed up to the door that led to the cells. I was getting strip-searched when a cop asked me, "What type of pills did you give Howard?"

Howard was a 16 year old who was in love with Wanda. Wanda had beat him up when he tried to press himself on her.

"What are you talking about?" I asked angrily as I pulled on my clothes.

"You gave him some pills. Then you and Wanda beat him up, took his money and clothes, and threw him in the snow."

"Get serious!" I was steamed. "What would I be doing with a snot-nosed kid like him? He probably tried to commit suicide. He's so madly in love with Wanda that he's ready to die for her."

As it turned out, he'd taken a stack of phenobarbs with straight whisky, then he'd taken off all his clothes but his undershorts and fallen asleep in a snow bank. That's where the police found him, and that's when he came up with this story about Wanda and me.

"We'll have to check it out. In the meantime, you're staying the night."

I glared at him. "You motherfucking pig!"

"You got a problem?"

"You're fuckin' right I do!" I threw my coat at him. "You're the problem! This is bullshit and you know it! You've been hassling me for the past three years, for anything, and you throw shit like this on me every chance you get. That's the problem! So fuck off! Just stay away from me!" I walked to the cells, leaving them in stunned silence. In a few seconds they gathered their wits enough to come and lock me in.

I was let out at six-thirty in the morning. I don't know how much "checking out" they'd done since eleven-thirty last night, but it must have been enough to clear me. I wished them all a Merry Christmas as I walked out the back door.

Things weren't over with Howard. Since he was so in love with Wanda, she'd mark him in for his car. I'd sold my own car two months before, so it came in handy from time to time. One night we drove to Regina and cruised Albert Street drinking beer. We left Howard in the car once while we went into a bar. He waited patiently for his love. I finally got him to have a few beers, and with Wanda's coaxing he even let me drive. It was about seven in the morning when Howard, who had passed out after five beer, woke up in the back seat screaming that Wanda didn't love him any more, that she was in love with me, and he wanted me to step outside and fight for her.

We were at a busy intersection. I sat shaking my head as Howard walked around the car, hollering and cursing. He kicked the headlights out and was starting on the tail lights before we could stop him. It was truly embarrassing as amazed and bewildered motorists detoured around our car, which had three doors open and the emergency lights flashing, while a girl comforted a drunken kid at the side of the street. I tried to make it less embarrassing by lifting the hood, only to have good Samaritans stopping to ask if I needed a hand. After a while we got him back in the car and roared away.

I wanted to smash Howard's face. The guy had told the cops a bunch of lies, and that made me wonder what else he'd told them. He was a racist, too. He believed I was beneath him in every category. I wanted to do to him what he'd told the cops I had done to him. But Wanda always told me to cool it. "He's got a car, Jim, so he has a purpose, a use for us. Let it slide." So I bit my tongue.

We returned to Fort Qu'Appelle about eleven o'clock in the morning. We weren't in town more then 10 minutes before the flashing red lights halted our progress once again. They grabbed Wanda and Howard, but not me. Surprise.

It took the better part of the afternoon to put the facts together: apparently Wanda had sold some stolen clothes to Howard's sister. Howard's sister had taken them to the police, told them where she'd got them and where they could find more, and then told them that her brother had stolen their father's car. Now both of them waited in jail while the police sorted out the facts. In the end Howard was exonerated and Wanda was remanded on four more counts of theft under $200, plus six counts of breach of probation.

The next night I was drinking scotch when the door flew open and four police officers burst in. They had me with the goods. I had a case of stolen whisky, rum, and gin. An ex-con who had called me bro and good people had informed the police that I had the stuff over at Dale's. I was taken to the station and formally charged with breaking and entering. Within an hour I was released on a promise to appear. Next day I went to court, putting all my charges together for sentencing. I had my sentencing deferred for a week. I had close to $600 in my pocket and I was going to party before I went to jail. It was New Year's Eve.

PART TWO

Crime

JANUARY 7th, 1983

I awake on the floor at Dale's. Other people are sleeping on the couch, the beds, or slumped in chairs, snoring, clutching half-full bottles or burnt-out cigarettes. It's nine-thirty, and my destiny is in half an hour. I crack open one last beer. I walk around, careful not to step on the inebriated strewn about on the floor. I'd bought 10 cases of beer the previous night and found 10 people to help me drink it. Others came over to wish me luck: Walter the car thief from Lebret, Murray the local drug dealer, and a host of undesirables from the town and surrounding area.

I walk to the Legion Hall, where they hold court in Fort Qu'Appelle. It's only two blocks away. The morning air is crisp and full of ice crystals. I burp the morning's beer as I walk through the front doors. The police watch me intently as I sit in the second row waiting to be sentenced. I wave to Wanda, and crack a joke.

"The court calls James Tyman," the police officer acting as crown prosecutor calls over the crowd.

Time seems suspended while I gather my wits to stand up before the judge.

"James Tyman," the officer intones, "you stand charged with possession of a restricted drug, that being two tablets of lysergic synthetic diethylamide, more commonly known as acid. You have also been charged with taking a vehicle without the owner's consent, and on the same date impaired driving, and still on the same date breach of probation, and ... excuse me, Your Honor, also in relation to the restricted drug charge, Mr Tyman has been charged with another breach of probation, and also he has been charged with breaking and entering on December 27th of last year."

"Are you ready to plead today, Mr Tyman?" The judge looks disgusted.

"Yes, Your Honor." I stare into his eyes. "Guilty on all counts."

His eyes never leave mine as he hands down the sentence. "Nine months in the Regina Correctional Center for the breaking and entering charge. Thirty days concurrent for the breach of probation in relation to the restricted drug charge, and 30 days concurrent for the restricted drug charge. Also, 30 days concurrent for the other breach of probation charge, 30 days concurrent for taking a vehicle without the owner's consent, and 30 days consecutive for the impaired driving charge. Next case." He breaks eye contact to motion to the smiling police officer to take me into custody. It's all official now. I'm 19 years old and I'm going to jail.

I wasn't there to see Wanda get sentenced. Within two minutes I was handcuffed and in the back of the police car.

I sat in my cell remembering better days: the times I rode my bike into the hills with that dog, riding my horse, swimming at the local beaches when I was a kid. My father took us there, and after we were finished swimming he'd take us for a Popsicle. My sisters and I used to fight to see who got to go into the store to buy the Popsicles, since whoever went in usually got to keep the change. There were a few memorable Christmas days that came back to me, too, especially the time I got the hockey net. The kids two blocks away had also received a hockey net for Christmas, and every Saturday morning there'd be 10 or 12 kids hacking and checking each other for the right to be called road hockey champions of Fort Qu'Appelle.

"Hey Jim, your partner just got 30 days." It was one of the local cops.

"I bet that makes you excited enough to piss." I let out a roar of laughter.

"Jim, Jim, Jim." He was smiling and shaking his head. "That's not the way to be. You should be nice to authority when you go to jail, so you can get out faster."

"Fuck you, asshole!" I watched him depart.

Wanda returned about 30 minutes later, and I started singing my own version of a popular theme song from a movie: "They call me the Baaaandit! If your door is locked, I'll breeaak it! You all may haaaate me! But why does your daughter want to daaaate me! I bet you that ..."

"All right, Jim. That's enough!" Two stern-faced cops stood in the doorway. "If you keep it up, we'll put you in the drunk tank to sing all night!"

"Fuck off! We're going to Regina this afternoon!" They slammed the door. "They call me the baaaandit! If you meet a cop's wife, fuuuuck it!"

In Regina I would be dropped off at the jail and Wanda would be taken to the RCMP holding cells until a plane could fly her up to Pine Grove Correctional Center in Prince Albert. The van came about two-thirty. Half a dozen police officers, including the local chief, were there to give me one last look. "See you in the fall, Jim," the chief remarked.

It was true that my sentence totalled 10 months, which put my release date in October. But under the law you automatically get one third off your sentence for good behavior, providing you qualify. I guess the chief figured I wasn't going to qualify. I was going to prove him wrong.

On the highway we stopped for a van from Melville and Yorkton and took on another six prisoners for "The Hill." The ride was silent. No one talked but Wanda and me. It was winter, but there were nine people in the van and it was hot. The booze from last night was sweating out of me. I couldn't wait to get to jail and have a shower.

We turn off on a gravel road, and the van seems to be picking up speed. My heart is picking up speed. I can feel sweat forming on my back. I don't think it's the booze this time. I can see the correctional center in the distance. It's closing in fast. Just two months ago on TV they were doing a story on the alarming number of suicides that have taken place here. Suicide hasn't entered my mind lately, but I know that to get by in jail you have to be strong or you'll be found one morning hanging.

* * *

The Regina Correctional Center was the most unfeeling, violent, and desperate place I had ever come across. You didn't need a master's degree in sociology to see the desperation and hatred in people's faces. The jail was divided into four "units," all connected. The first one you encounter is the oldest and the most violent unit in all of Saskatchewan's correctional system. Knifings are common. Beatings come the same way as the afternoon soap operas: regularly and on time. Inmates mutilate themselves with razors, or with nails smuggled from the carpentry shop, or just by banging their heads against the wall till either they're dead or they've knocked themselves unconscious. Extortion is as common as insects. The smell of sweat, feces, urine, and dried blood fills my nostrils, clouding my already perplexed mind and emotions.

The unit I'm supposed to head for is Unit Four C and D. When I ask a harmless-looking guy about it, he smiles smugly. I figure out why when I walk into Unit Four C and D: it's for first-timers, "fish," virgins. I'm ushered to the back of Unit Four, where there are four bunk beds set up for overflow inmates. As I walk along I notice most of the inmates are younger than me, like that snot-nosed Howard. I'm shown my bunk and start going through the kit I was issued in the shower room: one very used towel, one comb, one toothbrush and toothpaste, one razor and shaving lotion, and a complete change of clothes.

Other inmates come by to check me out. Some of the bolder ones stop and chat. One kid of 16, his forearms a maze of criss-crossing scars, is very talkative. Within minutes I know his age, his home town, his place of birth, his grandma's ailments, his charges, and his release date. Finally he stops verbalizing long enough to ask me my name. I'm in no mood to talk to him. For one thing he's white, and white people are at the bottom of the social ladder in here. I'm not about to make friends with one of them. It could come back to haunt me.

After his performance, along comes an Indian of the same age and size. He's quick to point out that the honkies watch their step in here: "It's not like the street for them racist fuckers," followed by raucous laughter. I nod. This is different, I'm thinking. The honkies are the oppressed minority in here. Yep, this is a different world, all right.

I was quickly accepted among the inmates. I was a solid guy, good people, a bro to my fellow Indians who made up 75% of the unit's population. But the young white kid, Kelvin, was the range's punching bag. Everyone made snide remarks to him about his baby face, or the fact that he was going to get fucked in the ass if he was ever sent to main population, or that he didn't have enough guts to kill himself when he slashed up. He was offered assistance if he ever wanted to try it again.

"I'll slash your wrists for ya! Make sure you bleed to death this time, honky!"

"Come to my cell next time. I'll hang you and fuck you!"

It was always followed by loud, coarse laughter. I'd been expecting raw behavior, but the racism was blatant. "You stinking honky!" would erupt from a card game where both whites and Indians were playing. I'd wait for a fight, some retaliation from the honky. There was none. The white race was definitely on egg shells in Four C and D.

Unit Four C and D had its own gym time slot, its own weight room time slot, even its own time to pick up fresh clothing. It was the administration's way of keeping the first-timers away from the harder and more damaging influences of the repeat offenders and career criminals. I noticed the fear it struck among first-timers when a guard threatened to move them into the general population if they didn't comply with unit rules and the orders. It worked on me, for a while.

We had our own gym period four nights a week, and that gave me a chance to play floor hockey. I received thunderous cheers from the Indian congregation whenever I rammed a white person into the wall, the floor, the net, or up three rows into the bleachers. I was blowing off steam. I was always seething. I couldn't put my finger on it, but once my blood was pumping in a game I'd become obsessed with hurtling my 220 pound frame at anyone on the opposite team. The guards watched in delight when one inmate tried to harm another. That was acceptable. But I had to even the odds a few times, so I'd ram Indian boys into the walls, too, so the guards couldn't label me a racist.

I was assigned a job within a week of my arrival. I was to work in the carpentry shop. It started at eight-thirty and ended at three forty-five, with one hour off for lunch and two regulated, 15 minute coffee breaks. I was expecting stiff commands and harsh work. I thought of the beatings the guards could give you. I thought of the possibility of been shanked or piped. I thought of the rumors of prison rape. I had those fears when I walked in, but after a week I drew my own conclusions. A lot of the stuff you hear about jail does happen in the Regina Correctional Center. But for some strange reason I had the impression that I'd learn a trade, start a new life. I'd been tried, convicted, and sentenced; now I thought the system was going to train me, give me parole, and push me in the direction of a new life. I must have still been on acid when I was thinking up that scenario.

I walked to work on a cold January morning with thoughts of learning to be a carpenter, a new beginning. I waited eagerly for the shop boss to give me instructions, or a work project. I waited. And I waited. I spent two weeks waiting. Finally I resigned myself to making sure the other inmates had coffee and keeping the coffee area clean. After that I'd lean back in a chair, pull my baseball cap over my eyes, and catch a few winks.

* * *

The shop boss was a man in his later years who was obviously just waiting to retire — no hassles, no confrontations, just do what's necessary. I found a lot of staff with this attitude. Others were there only to aggravate you, to frustrate you, to make sure you hated every goddamn day you were there. Jail is full of bitter men, and that type of bull just ferments the bitterness inside a man. I guess it's their version of rehabilitation.

My shop boss was a walking ghost. He never said more than was necessary. He never rose from his desk unless it was necessary. One day he called me over to look at my progress report. He had filled in "good work habits"; I never did a thing in there. He had filled in "follows orders well"; he had never spoken to me in the three weeks I'd been there. Then near the bottom he had me down as a "sloppy dresser." I looked at him for an explanation, but he was busy staring into space. I shrugged and signed my name, confirming that I was a good worker who could follow orders but I needed guidance in dressing myself.

I got tired of the monotonous routine of the carpentry shop, so I put in a request to see the counselor. I went to see him about the same time I had my progress report. He was interested in getting me paroled, and asked me about it. I told him maybe. I was learning from other inmates that when you're only doing 10 months you're supposed to be solid and say, "I'll do my time." I'd have to do the entire 10 months on parole, or do seven months in jail and be released with no restrictions. The more I thought of that, the easier it became to think, "Fuck your parole. I'll do my time." Eventually I said it, too.

"Well, Jim, I'll contact your local police and get their opinion." I snorted with laughter. "You don't think that's a good idea?"

"They've come to the jail twice since I've been here, trying to get me to confess to crimes I've never heard about. I don't think they'll be keeping open arms for my return."

"Oh, I didn't know. Well, I'll still see." The couselor always talked with a cocky grin on his face. "If not, how about CTR?"

"What's that?"

"Community Training Residence. It's a halfway house for guys who aren't quite ready to be released from custody. The house enables you to look for work, and if you're planning to go to school, they'll let you live there. Do you have your grade twelve?"

"Yeah."

"That's a change. How did you get it?"

"Going to school. How else?"

"Most guys don't have grade twelve. Even fewer got it by graduating from school. You're one of the rare ones."

"I'm honored," I said. "Now how about getting me a job where I can use all my worthy talents, instead of sitting on my ass waiting to die."

"I'll have to see. What do you want to do?"

"Anything where I can keep busy. I hate doing nothing. I thought jail was a place where they busted your ass, or trained you for something."

"If you were in the pen you could get training," he said. "But this is a provincial institution, and there are no funds for it."

"Next time I'll make sure to tell the judge to give me pen time, so I can become a mechanic or something."

"You plan on coming back?"

"No, but if they're going to throw you in jail, they might as well give you something to hope for. You know, there are guys on our range asking other inmates for money so they can get their General Education Diploma. The province would rather spend thousands of dollars keeping you inside than give you $20 to help you write your grade twelve final."

"Write to the premier. See what he says."

"Ah, fuck you too."

His smirk disappeared. "Watch yourself, Tyman. I could charge you and ..."

"Don't be so ignorant. You're supposed to be a counselor. Why don't you write to the premier and tell him a few things?"

He stared hard at me for a moment, then changed the subject. "Let's talk about your history."

I sighed. It was no use trying to explain anything to him. He wasn't going to listen.

One afternoon I started banging on the barred gate that separated the counselor's office from the main prison. Then I rang the bell until he came out, red-faced, to demand an explanation.

"I want a job! I want a job where I can work and sweat and feel like I'm doing something useful!"

"Have you heard of requests?"

"Don't give me that bullshit!" I didn't flinch under his threatening gaze. "You're right here and I'm right here, so fire me or transfer me to another job. I want to work, Christian! There are guys here who don't want to work and you're forcing them to work, so don't give me the run-around about no jobs to be had."

"Okay, you're fired until further notice!" He turned and stalked back to his office, slamming the door.

Things could have been worse. At least now I could sleep in and watch television all day. And the counselor eventually did get me a job working in the greenhouse, planting flowers and vegetables that would later be transplanted into the gardens around the jail. There was only one problem: he didn't inform me when I was supposed to start. So one day I found myself being escorted to kangaroo court, the committee that handled internal discipline in the institution. Failing to report for work placement was the infraction.

"The counselor didn't tell me I had to report for work today," I pleaded to the discipline panel members.

"According to him, he informed you yesterday. Why didn't you report?"

"I'm telling you, he never let me know."

"Have a seat outside for a minute."

I sat in the hall, expecting that the counselor would be phoned and he would explain that he had made a note to phone the unit and had simply forgotten. They did phone him, but he confirmed his earlier report. I was speechless. The counselor had got his revenge on me for disturbing his afternoon. I had heard they did this type of stuff, but I didn't believe it till now. I was told that I could be charged with lying to staff members, but would be given a warning this time.

"Five days remission will be placed over your head," said the Assistant Deputy Director, "The Five," as he was called; I don't know why. It was just part of prison slang. "Further charges will result in your losing five days, plus new sanctions brought up at that time."

The next morning I walked to the greenhouse in plenty of time, sure that the counselor was just giving me another bogus job to shut my mouth for a while. I sat with the other inmates on the detail: two brothers who were doing two years less a day each for robbing a man on a busy Regina street, a quiet burnt-out Indian who obviously measured your gas tank with his lungs, and Larose the comedian, who kept everyone's ribs sore with his remarks about guards, politicians, churches, and of course white people.

I was pleased with the work. "That damn counselor came through," I thought to myself. I was pleased that I was doing something useful. We planted onions, tomatoes, flowers, and even some marijuana, but that was quickly discovered by the greenhouse boss. He surprised me by not firing the lot of us; he just told us to plant it in a better place next time.

Our shop boss was a good man. He kept us busy, and he'd sneak fresh pineapple from the kitchen for us every Friday afternoon. He talked to you as if you weren't an inmate but simply another human being. He was retiring in a year, but unlike the carpentry shop boss he wouldn't let you sit on your ass even if you were tired. If you didn't follow his rules, you were fired. He wasn't one to do meaningless work, either. He told us at coffee break one day how he'd just had a beef with the administration over some work project he concluded was absurd.

"They want to fire me, good for them," he said. "I'm getting out of here next year anyway. They can take their job and stuff it! What do you say to that, Larose?"

"Hail Messiah. You have spoken. It will be written."

I had one friend in there, an Indian from Meadow Lake who was doing two years less a day, the maximum for a provincial jail. He had 43 breaking and entering charges against him, so they gave him a break and ran every other charge concurrent after he received two years for the first. We went outside when the snow melted and played horseshoes or walked the track together. My first impression was that he was a hardcore racist, but after talking to him for a while I learned that I was the one who really was not informed. It was like meeting Lorne all over again, the Indian back at Bert Fox Composite High School who'd told me to get some Indian bros and quit hanging around with honkies. "Maybe you'll see what the truth really is," Lorne had said, and now, finally, I was ready to hear it. I had learned about Indians from white people. I hadn't bothered to question their analysis because I was afraid of rejection. After talking to Herbie about Indian people and their beliefs, I found that I was myself a hardcore racist. I felt disgusted with myself, remembering all the snide remarks I had made over the years about Indian people. They weren't a bunch of bloodthirsty savages. They were my own people. I hated my own people. My own people hated white people. I didn't know who I was or where I was going.

"You're an apple, Tyman," Herbie was quick to point out.

I wanted to ask him if he knew any Martins from Ile-à-la-Crosse. I thought that could be what I was looking for — the past I couldn't recall, a sense of identity, of who I really was. You can't take someone's past away and expect him not to miss it, or not to look for it. It was eating at my insides. Finally I did ask him, and he replied, "There's lots of Martins up there. Why? You related to them?"

"Uh, no. I just knew a couple. I was wondering if there were quite a few of them up there, that's all." I never told people I was adopted unless they saw my family, and then it became obvious. It was sure to prompt a horde of questions I couldn't answer. I wanted to avoid that lost feeling I had when someone asked me, "Who are you?"

I had been there two months when the counselor sent word up to the unit that he wanted to see me. I went to his office. He had his smirk in place. "Jim, how about going to CTR?"

"When?" I felt excited. I could get out on the street and see people.

"You're appealing your sentence, aren't you?"

I was appealing the sentence for the simple reason that it got me out of jail for a day. "I go up in two weeks. Why?"

"We can't do anything till your court appearance is dealt with."

"Oh."

"I see what you mean about the police in your town." He broke formation and looked serious. "They object strongly to your release there. They say you're a menace."

"Parole is out of the question, then."

"I would say so. Your mother says she can't control you, and the community would rather see you on TV than on the street, if you know what I mean. The best alternative is to get you to the halfway house in Regina."

I told him that would be fine with me. He handed me an application and told me he'd be in touch. Three days later he told me I was accepted, but I had to wait for the court decision concerning my appeal.

March 14th was the date of my appeal. It was beginning to cause me sleepless nights. I was more than a little upset with my sentence after learning that other inmates were doing only six months for their third break and enter.

I had made contact with a lawyer who ran a small organization of work projects for ex-cons and who had in fact been a con himself before taking hold of his life and becoming a lawyer. I wanted to ask him how he'd done it, but when he was interviewing me he never once looked at me. He'd ask questions and scribble down my replies. He left telling me not to worry, I'd win my appeal. I didn't see him again till I walked into appeal court.

I sat through the whole session. Everyone who went up got some time knocked off his original sentence. My lawyer was also representing three others, and he was doing a whale of a job. Hell, I thought, if I was one of the judges I'd probably be giving his clients money and a place to live, let alone a lighter sentence. Finally it was my turn to enter the little box below the judges' podium.

"Your Lordships, James Tyman has just recently turned 19 years old. This is his first incarceration. James has informed me that he was a meat-cutter for nine months, and hopes to go to school to continue his training. James is also a talented football player and has received offers to try out with the Saskatoon Hilltops organization. As you can see, Mr Tyman's release date is set for the end of July. I have been in contact with the organization to find out their starting dates for training camp. As a rookie, Mr Tyman would have to report at the beginning of July, since that is the date set for newcomers. I would also like to point out to your Lordships that the usual sentence for first-timers on a breaking and entering charge is from three to six months. I feel Mr Tyman's sentence is harsh, and would ask the court for compassion in light of these facts. Thank you."

I felt this had all been rehearsed before I got here, including my lawyer's bullshit about the Saskatoon Hilltops. The three judges looked at each other, they nodded, and I was told to stand up. "Mr Tyman, the court is merciful and understanding. Your nine-month sentence for breaking and entering will be reduced to six months. Dismissed."

I walked down the narrow flight of stairs to the holding cells where a jubilant bunch of cons were celebrating their good fortune. I could hear them behind the steel door, slapping each other on the back and planning their futures. I guess it was then that I realized where I really was. I saw two names carved into the wall, and recognized both of them right away. One had just received a life sentence for killing a local prostitute; the other had just received a life sentence in a well-publicized trial for the murder of a university professor. This was the real thing.

I told the counselor about my victory in court. "Really!" He had a look of astonishment. "Well, I'll get hold of CTR and we'll get you out of here as fast as possible. How's that?"

I walked onto the range shouting, "Justice has been done! We live in a free society where fairness and honesty are put on a pedestal! We the people should be ..."

"Ah, shut the fuck up!" an Indian from Alberta spoke up.

"Just because you're dogging it, doesn't mean I am," I said. "So go lock yourself in your drum and write poetry."

He gave me a half smile. "You won your appeal, I take it."

"Justice has been done!" I raised my hands in true preacher fashion and walked down the range, telling everyone my new release date.

My enthusiastic entrance did not in the least impress Gord Farrow, our little general. He was one of the regular guards, and his sole purpose was to ensure that before he got off his shift someone would be pulling his hair out in frustration over some act he had pulled. He looked daggers at me as I went singing around the range, telling everyone that the justice system was fair and honest. He was going to carry the flame of his own justice and deliver the message from the correctional center.

It was Saturday morning two days after I came back from my appeal when Farrow came barging into my cell. "Tyman! You're locked up for sleeping in!" I rolled over and sighed. I knew my release was soon and I didn't want to screw it up because of one man's ignorance. I closed my eyes and made myself relax.

But Farrow wasn't done with me. The following week I slept late. I jumped to my feet, throwing my clothes on. I raced to the gate. It was open from 8:20 to 8:30 to let us out for work. I got there at 8:28, but according to Farrow I was too late. He placed me on charge for sleeping in. He was giggling when he slammed the gate, and still giggling when he handed me the charge sheet. "Justice has been done, Tyman. Justice has been done." I was placed on room confinement till the disciplinary panel could hear my case the next day.

I almost hooked that five-foot-eight-inch bag of hot wind. But my instincts told me I was headed for a world of trouble if I laced this guy. We did have one guard who was more than willing to take you on. It was simple: you wanted a fight, he would oblige, and there would be no administration problems after. He had a handful of black belts, and he never smiled unless he was belittling you. General Farrow was just the opposite: he insulted you and degraded you till you swore at him or, like Kelvin finally did one day, took a swing at him. Then he'd scoot like a spooked mouse to his office and dial for help. Soon the goon squad would come and haul your carcass to the hole, all because this guy had an attitude problem.

I walked to kangaroo court resigned to saying nothing, for the simple reason that it did no good.

"Three days remission lost." The Five put on his best threatening face for me. "I suggest you get up in the morning from now on."

One day I had a few choice comments for Farrow, who threatened to move me off the unit and into main population. I laughed at him, and that made him madder. Then he turned to answer the phone ringing in his office.

"The counselor wants to see you, Tyman," he spat.

"Well, Jim," said the counselor, "you go to CTR tomorrow."

The halfway house was located in a lower-class area of Regina between Albert and Broad Streets, two blocks from the YMCA. I didn't know it at the time, but a few of my old schoolmates were boozing it up and dealing drugs a block and a half away. It was convenient.

The first person I saw was the former owner of the café from my home town, the same café where my parents used to take us after church. She was the cook at the halfway house. She recognized me right away, and was visibly surprised to see me in a house for cons.

"You were such a good boy, Jimmy," she said in her heavy Greek accent. "Your papa was such a good man, and your mama was such a nice lady. Jimmy, Jimmy, you stay outta trouble."

I was confined to the house the first night, as per policy, but the second day I awoke with a sense of excitement and expectancy. I was allowed out for the entire day to look for work. I never looked for work those first two days. I just walked the Cornwall Center mall in downtown Regina. It felt odd to see all these people, and not some desperate cons. All I could think about was jail and what my fellow cons were doing back in The Hill. Now that I was out, I knew I was different from other people. I'd come from a place few have been, and fewer know what it is really all about. "Come on Jim," I kept telling myself. "You were only there three months. Forget it and start fresh." But I kept thinking that everyone knew I was a criminal. They wouldn't give me a chance.

When I did look for work my old fears were there instead of my new ones. I was met with cold stares or stunned expressions when I asked for work. "Well, I don't know, really. How about filling out this application and we'll give you a call?" I knew what they were thinking. Being an ex-con wasn't my problem. My problem was that I was an Indian.

I contacted my old chum Terry who was living with his mother. I felt companionship with him more then ever now. We understood each other. We talked briefly about my incarceration, but it was more of a silent conversation. I mentioned the racism and he nodded his understanding. I mentioned the bulls, and he nodded. He mentioned the filth, and I nodded.

What did it all mean? Besides being marked for life, what was the meaning of it? Who benefited? Who jumped with joy at my incarceration? Is society better? Am I better?

Terry was more deeply involved in drugs; in fact he was dealing. Within a few minutes he was passing me some magic mushrooms. They grow wild in British Columbia and have the same effect as acid. Within half an hour I was tripping, hallucinating, my body in a cold sweat. We went over to my old schoolmates' apartment near the halfway house. They were surprised to see me out so soon. "What did you do? Escape?" They thought that was really funny. They told me that my name had been in the newspapers back home, with a list of my sentences. I was drinking cold beer and tripping badly when another old buddy came in — one of the guys I'd partied with over Easter when Rachael hung her underwear on the light fixtures and Tom accused me of stealing his teeth. It turned out that a lot of townspeople knew about my release to the halfway house. Someone was keeping tabs on me, because I hadn't told anyone.

I had visions of staying and partying. Terry was telling me I'd only get "another 30 days, big deal" if I didn't go back. I was tempted, but my instincts got a grip on the situation and I turned down the next offer of beer and said my good-byes.

The next day the staff at the halfway house got me a temporary job, along with another con. We were sent to a new residential area on the northwest side of Regina. Our job was to unload kitchen cabinets for apartment buildings. It was back-straining work. To help matters, it was raining.

I got to know the con I was working with. As it turned out, he knew Terry. He'd been over at his house buying MDA just last night. He was well built from years of prison life, which was common among guys who did lots of time. He told me he never spent much time on the street: a few months at the most, then it was back inside for a few months or a few years, depending on the charges. He took it in stride. He didn't seem bitter about the merry-go-round life he was leading. He discussed it with me like a lawyer discusses cases with an associate.

The job lasted two days. After that I went to the Casual Labor Office on Broad Street. I got a job the first day, at a church in south Regina. There, along with six others, all of them straight johns, I filled five-gallon pails with cement, hauled them downstairs, and poured them into a form. One of the pillars holding up the main floor of the building had shifted, and we were in the process of building another. If the kitchen cabinet job was hard, this was torturous. My arms were screaming by the end of the day. My back felt permanently bent. "You guys meet me at the Casual Labor Office tomorrow at eight and there'll be more work," the church's maintenance man announced at the end of the day.

I went back the next morning. I was still sore from last night, but I wanted to work. I was filled with thoughts of the maintenance man hiring me full time after he saw how hard a worker I was. But at noon he announced that a professional contractor had been given the go-ahead to finish the job. Thanks, guys.

I spent the afternoon in the Cornwall Center mall watching the local drug dealers plying their trade. "I should be doing that," I whispered to myself. Why should those guys be making money the easy way while I busted my ass for a church full of phonies? I pondered these thoughts. Half of me wanted to sell drugs and take it easy; the other half wanted to work and go to school and learn a trade. I walked the mall till it was time to go back for supper. That night I went to see Terry. He sold me a bag of dope and offered me some MDA.

"Want to try a fix?"

"No, man. That shit is bad for you, sticking needles in your arm. I'll stick to dope."

I believed what I was saying then. The next morning I went back to the mall and sat with a couple of cons from the house having coffee. I was walking back for dinner when who should I run into but my little Indian friend, Lorne. He was sitting in Victoria Park smoking dope with a person unknown to me. He looked like a sniffer, one of the guys who got little pity in jail.

They did it to themselves.

"Well, Tyman, how's it going?" He motioned for me to sit beside him and his spaced-out friend.

"Not bad. Where have you been? It must be four, five years since last time I saw you."

"Actually, it's been about three weeks."

I looked at him, puzzled.

"I've been in jail with you, up on One D. I saw you go by with the kids' range when you went to movie night."

"Well I'll be a son of a bitch. That means you're a repeater."

He grinned broadly. "Sixth time inside."

"Six times! You aren't that old!"

"Hey, it's life. You'll find out soon enough." He handed me the last half of the joint. "Here, Tyman. I gotta go. See you in jail."

I took a big puff of the joint. I looked around at all the straight johns. "I'm not like you guys. I'm a con."

Moose Jaw flashed back to me: the street, the people, the drugs and money, the respect, the power. I'd wanted it then, and now I was going to get it. But not from doing odd-jobs from a halfway house in Regina.

I went to see the director. "Take your CTR program and stick it."

"Pack your bags, then." He was mad. "You're going back to the center this afternoon!"

The escorting officer was shaking his head as we drove through Regina back to the center. "Jesus Jim. Why didn't you stick it out? You only had seven weeks to go, then you were out. Why would anyone want to go back into that place?"

"You get used to it after a while," I replied nonchalantly. I was more interested in watching the girls in their shorts in the warm April weather.

"That's not right, Jim. You should hate jail, not like it."

I turned from the people on the street. "I said you get used to it. I didn't say I liked it. It's guys like you who want us to hate it, and most of you make sure that we do. You're the ones who cause the problems in there."

The admitting officer suggested to the escorting officer that I should lose 30 days for being sent back.

"What would that prove?" I asked.

"Then maybe guys like you would be more grateful for these opportunities!"

"I came back on my own, pal. The program is a good one, but I'm not going to bullshit anyone by staying there taking up bed space someone else could use."

"You're headed for a world of trouble, Tyman." He looked right at me. "I'll be seeing you again and again."

I was welcomed back to unit Four C and D by a horde of comments and questions.

"What happened? Couldn't handle it?"

"Nah, it's for people like you." I smiled.

"Whadda you mean?"

"You know, the phonies who know the game and want to play it. Oh, I'm cured. Praise the Lord. Take me to the halfway house."

"Fuck that, Tyman! I'm no phony."

"Neither am I. That's why I'm back."

Within two days I was given a job with a crew that worked downtown every day. It was a crew everyone wanted to get on, and the guards knew it. We were taken to the exhibition grounds to rake the lawns. I wasn't there more than 10 minutes when the crew boss, a man who never left the van and who had a stack of salami-on-rye beside him, called me over.

"Jim, I noticed you're not working."

"What do you mean, not working? I've been keeping up with everyone else."

"I see that, but why are you talking to everyone while you work? Don't you know you're slowing them down?"

"You mean you don't want any talking."

"Well, Jim, we stop for coffee and smoke breaks. You can conspire with anyone you want then."

"All I'm doing is talking while I work."

"I won't repeat myself. You work and don't bother the other inmates and I won't have to fire you."

I left the van biting my tongue. I wanted to tell the fat slob to take his wonderful job and stick it. But it was nice to get out of the smelly jail for the day.

"What did he want?" a veteran whispered, not breaking his raking motion.

"He says I'm influencing you hardened criminals not to work. Didn't anyone tell him I'm the fish" — the first-timer, another bit of prison slang — "and you guys are the bad influence?"

He let out a muffled laugh. "You're the bad influence, Tyman. You're supposed to bow to them for giving you this opportunity to work in the community."

"I'll steal his stack of sandwiches," I said. "Then he'll have something to bitch about." Two other inmates joined in the muffled laughter.

It was close to noon when I was waved to the van once again. The stack of sandwiches was half depleted, and the crew boss was just screwing the cap back on an extra large thermos. "Jim, you're still up to it. Quit talking while you work."

"Come off it, pal. I'm doing the job, aren't I?"

"Well, yes, you are. But you're not complying with my instructions." He let out a burp that smelled of salami and coffee.

"Why is it me who's getting the speech? I do believe I'm not the only one talking out there."

"Exactly, and you're the reason why. I'm not going to warn you again, Jim. Work and be silent. Don't conspire and influence."

I left the van again biting my tongue. "What a prick," I whispered.

"They're just riding your ass because you came back from CTR and you're supposed to ..."

"To bow and give thanks. I know, I know." I sighed.

After dinner we were working by the east gate when the van

took off to the other side of the parking lot, about 150 yards away.

"What d'you think he's up to?" an inmate whispered, never breaking stride. He was well trained.

"Probably waiting for the delivery truck to bring him a side of beef to get him through the afternoon."

We continued raking for 20 minutes, then one of the prison cars pulled up beside the van. After a brief exchange it headed in our direction. When it stopped the driver motioned me over.

"What's up?" I played the duck.

"I don't know. I just got a call to come out here, so here I am." He was very cool. "Get in." I jumped in the front seat and the car roared away.

"West G, Tyman. What you think of that?" The admitting officer was smiling.

"Well, sir." I bowed. "May the good Lord bless you on Judgment Day." He motioned to the escorting guard to get me out of his sight.

"You're a smart-ass, Tyman," my escort commented — after we got through the first steel door, so his comrade wouldn't hear his laughter.

I was ushered to the end of the range. Down here was where most of the inmates waited for their 30 day appeal, then they were sent to the pen. I lay on my stained mattress, inclined just to finish my time off right here, away from the egotistical guards, away from the role-playing inmates, away from the hatred, away from the racism. I drifted off to sleep watching a soap opera through the bars. I was awakened by a guard rattling the bars with his keys. "Come on, Tyman. Charge panel."

"Already? I just got back an hour ago." I wiped the sleep out of my eyes as I followed him up to the main floor and my return engagement with the court.

"Well, Tyman, you just can't handle being in the community long, can you?" The Five wore a scowl.

"Do you think I was born and raised in jail?" I asked. "Hell, I just got to learn how to give thanks."

"It has nothing to do with that! It's the way you conduct yourself. The crew boss asked you twice to comply with instructions to work and you were sarcastic and showed no restraint. So you've been charged with failure to perform work duties. You will be confined for five days." He motioned to the guard to take me back to West G.

After five days I was escorted back to Four C and D, and found my stay very enjoyable. Two minutes later I was being whisked off the range into One F, without a word. Five minutes later the guard came back. This time I was taken down to One D. Again I was confined to my cell, but this time the guard at least told me something: that he was "following orders."

I felt the atmosphere immediately. There were no tentative inmates in One D; there was no joking around. This was serious. I lay on my bunk wondering what I was being locked up for. My five days' confinement were over. It was near noon when the guard came down the range to open my cage.

I studied the inmates, and they studied me. I couldn't get over the filth. Ketchup had been sprayed on the wall in who knows what decade; there was some type of life form growing on it. The shower room stung the nostrils and the eyes; it was littered with discarded shorts that no one bothered or dared to pick up. The only decent thing about the range was the windows that looked out into the parking lot, where every Sunday inmates would line up looking for their weekly visits. I never had a visit while I was there. My mother and my brother Bill wanted to come, and Barry Dick, a childhood friend who had changed his last name and was now a radio personality. But they were straight johns and I wanted nothing to do with them. I saw them as the enemy now. In the life I was headed for they couldn't be anything else.

I was informed of my work placement the next day. I was to go back to the greenhouse, the reasoning being that it was the only place where I had "followed the program." The boss shook his head when I told him of my experiences in the past two weeks.

"You should have stayed put, Tyman. I would have looked after you."

"I should have. At least you act human."

He nodded. He knew what I was talking about. Anyone who does time will tell you that a little respect and trust will make the wheels of incarceration run smoothly. Unfortunately, there are guards who like to create potholes and bumps which result in problems, which result in the inmate resenting the guards and the guards complaining to the administration that the inmates are abusive and should be confined or charged. So the merry-go-round continues — riots, murders, escapes, hostage-takings, suicide, self-mutilation. Seeing the nameless faces with carved-up arms, some with carved-up throats, made me hard. When one excited con would shout down the range that so-and-so had just slashed up, the rest of us who sat playing cards would reply nonchalantly, "Yeah, really?" and the game would go on. The victim would be forgotten by next hand. The guards didn't care, either. They had seen it countless times — "Yeah, really?" — and 10 minutes later they'd have to be reminded by The Five to get someone to mop up the blood. "What for? Oh yeah, I forgot."

The last month of my stay I was extremely restless. I'd be watching television, then halfway into a program I'd get up and start reading a book. Ten pages into the book and I'd be off to gaze out the windows, staring blankly at Regina's flickering lights, wondering who was getting drunk, who was getting stoned, who was getting loved, who would join us tomorrow.

I talked to few people on One D. They knew I was a fish, but they soon discovered that I was a solid guy and they left me to myself. One F was just above us. It had the catwalk, just like my soldier-of-fortune cell-mate had described it, and he was right about the guys who were too scared to come down to watch TV. One F was mostly occupied by honkies, so it was unwise to venture off the range unless you had friends in population or the reputation of a solid guy.

Kelvin was up on One F. He ventured down a few times, only

to have the older inmates vying for the right to be his "dad," or his protector. One thing about that, though: the kid had a choice, and Kelvin made his. He'd come down to make his dad toast and bring him coffee in the evening. Kelvin had carved his arms to shreds while he was inside, and while I was gone to CTR he'd flipped out in his cell on the fish range and was escorted off to One F, where he had to be handcuffed to the bars because he was taking runs like a ram at the bars, trying to open up his head. After 30 minutes he was injected with a sedative. Then he settled down. The handcuffs were removed, and he was told that if he tried it again he was going to the hole. There he'd die, and they'd carry him out after the insects had had their fill and when they could find the time.

I am working in the garden, planting onions every inch in a row the length of a football field. I feel like bitching to the boss, but I know what his reply will be: "Get off my crew, then." I don't need any more trouble. I've only got two weeks left.

I'm just getting used to my new cell and routine when off I'm hustled again, and again there's no explanation. This time I go to North G in the basement. North G is usually reserved for the drunks and winos who are in for 30 to 60 days for beating up their wives or writing bad checks. People never stay long, so the place doesn't get looked after. If Regina is a hole, North G is a hole in the hole. You have to make sure to look in the shower before you go in, so you won't step on a family of insects. You wake up in the night to see them scooting across the floor toward the butter and honey you laid down for them, if you were smart. You check your shoes in the morning for them. You check your food if you leave it for a minute to wash your hands.

It's the day before my release and I'm walking on my toes. I pace constantly. I wonder what awaits me. I have no solid plans. I plan to get out of Fort Qu'Appelle — that's on the top of my list. I plan to drink till I drop. I plan to find a woman. I plan to hit the streets and find my people. I know they're out there. They told me where. Now it's my turn for action.

MAY 28TH, 1983

I awoke at seven in the morning, fully dressed, lying on top of the blankets. I had never before woken up so full of life. At eight-thirty the prison van came to escort us downtown to the bus depot to begin our new beginning. I was still only 19 years old.

I watched the people walking to work, going shopping, or just headed for early morning gossip on coffee row. We turned off Victoria Avenue. The faded 10 foot sign of the bus depot came into view. The van rolled to a stop in front of the main doors. Eight of us jumped out, faces beaming with excitement, toting our prison issue suitcases — black garbage bags — with all our worldly possessions. I was first to the ticket window. I purchased a locker key, threw in my clothes, locked the door and left the depot amid the stares and whispered comments of the travelers.

I walked to the Cornwall Center and took up my position along the second floor railing, watching the morning people. I fumbled through some papers I had, addresses and phone numbers of people I'd met inside. "Yeah, Jimmy. Come see me. We'll pull a few scores and party all night long." Or my favorite: "Yeah, Tyman. You hit the streets, come and see me. I'll get you a whore. I'll get you stoned and drunk, and together we'll make lots of money and fuck the world!"

It was about eleven-thirty when I gave Barry a call. "He's not here now," a very sweet voice replied to my question. "Who's calling?"

"Jim Tyman. Barry told me to give him a call when I" — I hesitated — "when I got back into town."

"Oh, it's you. I know where you've been, Jimmy," she said playfully. "You've been a bad boy, haven't you?"

I played along. "Not me. All I ever did was steal hubcaps to get money for my poor old granny with the heart condition."

She laughed. "Barry said you were funny. Why don't you come over and tell me a few jokes, and we'll see if you're as big as Barry says you are." She giggled. "If you know what I mean."

"I can handle that."

She told me the address, and said she'd have something for me to eat also. "Come on, Tyman. The oven is getting warm already."

She was an Indian girl named Devonne. She was getting ready for what she called her octane boost. She was fixing talwin — or winnies, as they're called on the street. "Do you want to try a fix, Jimmy?"

"No thanks, and call me Jim."

"Sure ... Jim." She smiled. "I wish I had some Rs." She was talking about ritalin. "Want to go with me to get some Rs, Jimmy — whoops — Jim?"

"I got some things I want to do. Tell you what, I'll give you a call tomorrow."

She looked disappointed. "Why don't you stay with me for the day? I can make us some money and we can party the night away. Isn't that what you boys from jail like to do?"

"Sure, but I made promises to see other people today. You know how it is."

"Yes, I know how it is. But you must know how it is with me, too. There are more Jimmy Tymans out there, and a lonely lady might just forget which one she talked to the night before and take the wrong one home."

"I understand." I got up and put on my coat. "Do you want me to give you a call tomorrow anyway?"

She fixed her winnies, closing her eyes as the drug raced up her vein. She applied a piece of tissue paper to stop the trickle of blood on her arm. "Sure, give me a call, Jimmy. I'm home till three most days. If not, come over and wait for me." Her voice was slow. She was beginning to slur her words.

"Great, Devonne." I walked to the door. "Thanks for dinner."

"Any time, Jimmy. Any time." I shut the door and walked down the street. We hadn't eaten a thing.

I walked back to the Cornwall Center and went into the Elephant and Castle. There were mostly business people dressed in suits having an afternoon cocktail with a client, their secretary, or drowning some defunct business deal. I ordered a rye and Coke, and sipped it thinking of Devonne's proposition. It was an easy way to make money, but the violence that goes with having a prostitute worried me.

"Hey, bro, tansi," a smiling Indian said from three stools down.

"Sorry pal, I don't speak Indian. But how the fuck are you?" The rye was already making me feel good.

"You're not Sioux?"

"I'm Métis."

"Well, bonjour monsieur." His laughter sounded like cackling.

"Ah, oui monsieur." I laughed along with him.

"What's your name, brother?"

"James Tyman."

"Well hello, Jimmy Tyman. My name is Ivan Blackfeather."

"I'd be more pleased to meet you if you bought me another rye and Coke. But if you want my undivided attention, buy me a double."

He grinned. "Bartender, get this man a double of your finest whisky, and bill me."

We spent the afternoon talking about politics, religion, white people, black people, Indian people, all types of people and things. Ivan had been a school teacher at one of the reserves around Fort Qu'Appelle, but had one problem aside from not being able to teach: he drank too much. I didn't realize how much too much until he took me to a house downtown to meet some of his friends.

"I'd like you to meet my good friend Jimmy Tyman." Ivan had one hand on my shoulder, and the other raised high to grab the moment for my introduction. I looked around the shabby room. Battered furniture was strewn about, some with children huddled up on it, looking suspiciously at me.

"You want a drink?" The woman had murky, lost-looking eyes.

"Yeah, sure." I reached for the wine bottle. I wasn't much of a wine drinker but I didn't want to upset my hosts. I took a hefty swallow. My throat caught fire. "Jesus Christ! What is this?" I stared at the bottle. The people in the room, including the children, burst into laughter.

"It's Lysol, my good friend." Ivan spoke over the laughter. "You must not be used to it."

"Go have some water in the kitchen," the woman said. "You'll feel better then."

I gulped down gallons of water. The Lysol was burning my mouth, my throat, my stomach. Back in the living room they were passing around the wine bottle full of watered disinfectant. I watched in disbelief as one of the children took a big gulp. He smiled triumphantly and passed it on to his auntie. "She's in the wheelchair from drinking too much of this stuff," Ivan whispered to me. They had to pull the jug away from her. She started crying like a baby, so they let her have one more swallow. I shook my head and walked out. No one noticed.

I decided to give my old buddy Terry a call. He said he'd meet me at the Cornwall Center. I waited for him in the bar. I was smiling and laughing when he came through the door.

"Looks like you're enjoying your freedom."

I laughed loudly and slapped him on the back. "So where's all your drugs?"

"They're in my pocket. You want to get high?"

"Damn right. Let's go to the park and blow a few and I'll tell you jail stories."

"I've heard them all."

We spent the supper hour getting high and reminiscing. Terry wanted to know my plans for the future. I thought of Devonne and her plans. Terry suggested that I sell drugs through the downtown bars, since I liked bars and I could mix well with that scene. "Or maybe you should be a pimp, Jim. You're big and rank enough." He hesitated. "That's what you're going to do, isn't it."

"Maybe I'll muscle in on your drug business." He snorted

with laughter. "You never know, pal. This is the street. I'm a criminal and so are you. We go by the law of the jungle."

Terry looked serious. "A dog-eat-dog world, eh Jim?"

"Jail taught me a lot."

"Like how to be more violent?"

"A little of that, and a little about life on the streets."

"You going to be one of the boys from downtown?"

"I'm just going to be me. No one holds me. No one controls me. If someone gets in my way, chances are one of us is going to die."

"You're crazy, man." Terry shook his head and looked away.

"It's life, pal. No more bullshit. You should know what I'm talking about. Look at those phony assholes in jail who play macho men and tough guys. They go around robbing old people and beating up their so-called friends, taking their welfare checks after they pass out. Those guys are bullshit. And yet they're always talking about selling drugs and running whores downtown. All they do is draw heat for everyone else. Most of them are stool pigeons who should be buried."

"You're going to be a bad-ass, aren't you?" Terry asked quietly.

"More than likely."

"Who would figure it, a former church-going Indian running for mayor of the downtown scene."

"I told you, I'm not going to be involved with that."

"That's where you're headed, Tyman. You're just like those guys from downtown — to hell with everybody and everything."

"What do you have going for you?"

"Hey, pal!" Terry's face went hard. "I've got a good business selling drugs, and as a matter of fact I plan on going to university next year."

"You're leading a double life, then. I go one way. I don't associate with any straight arrows."

"What about your old friends from town?"

"They're country boys. Fuck them."

Terry smiled faintly. "Good luck then, Jim, in your quest to kick the ass of everyone you don't like."

"If it was everyone I didn't like I'd go on a rampage through Fort Qu'Appelle."

"You've got a lot of bad feelings from that town, don't you?"

I glared at him. "You should know."

"I know how it was, Jim. But I'm not saying to hell with the world because of a few bad years in Fort Qu'Appelle."

"Neither am I," I shot back.

"Well, it looks like you got a hard-on for life because of your bad feelings about the way people treated you."

"What are you, my psychiatrist? I was born criminal, I guess."

"Sure thing, Jim. You were born bad." We exchanged silent glances before he spoke up. "Let's go see one of your former straight-arrow friends. Kent's in town looking for work. He's got a room down by Wascana. Want to go?"

"What the hell, at least he smokes dope. And Terry, I was a bad boy in town, remember, so I'll tell you, he's not so straight." He shot a glance at me, and we both laughed.

I bought a case of beer and we walked the six blocks to Kent's apartment. Kent was stoned already, and after an hour of smoking dope and drinking beer and Southern Comfort I was getting rowdy. Kent suggested we go to Fort Qu'Appelle. I was all for it. He phoned a preppy buddy of his who had a car. When the guy came over he was wide-eyed to see this big drunk Indian, and I started joking about what would happen to his manhood if he ever went to jail. Kent and Terry laughed along with me, but the guy was visibly upset. He kept scowling in my direction. Bad mistake. We decided to cruise the city for a while in his new car. When he still wouldn't stop looking daggers at me I let him know what I thought of his disposition. I put a fist through his windshield. He was aghast. I laughed in his face. He demanded I pay for it. I told him sure, just take me out to my reserve where I have lots of money. He didn't like that idea. He demanded that I show him my license. I shrugged, no problem. It doesn't mean much unless you verify you showed him your license and sign your name. I watched him write down the information. I looked at Kent, who was smiling and shaking his head. After ten minutes of the guy almost breaking down over his windshield he threw us out of the car. We were left holding the beer on a busy downtown street. Kent made another call to another friend. This time he made sure it was someone I knew and got along with, since it was obvious I was in a wild mood.

By the time we got to Fort Qu'Appelle I was even wilder. We went to Echo Valley Park. There were about 10 of us pouring back the beer when along came two uniformed park security officers. They started to complain about the noise we were making. Then they spotted me and they demanded that we leave the park. I grabbed a burning log from the fire and started after them. They turned and fled. I threw the log at their departing car, warning them never to come back or I'd roast their balls.

My buddies stood wide-eyed. They knew I was rowdy but this bordered on criminal. We went to another beach. My blood was pumping. I was looking for a fight. I smashed a beer bottle and challenged the congregation to a brawl. They took off, leaving me with just my faithful buddy Francis, who shook his head and told me to throw that damn bottle away or he was going to beat the shit out of me. I jumped up at the challenge, but he never flinched. We stood eying each other, and I gave in. I threw the jagged bottle away. I sat down, realizing what had just taken place. I was losing my mind. I wanted blood and more blood. I wanted to hurt people. I wanted to cause them as much pain as their racism had caused me.

Francis and I cruised around town, drinking beer and reminiscing. About one o'clock I decided to go home and see my mother. I thought she wouldn't have been in bed so long that she wouldn't wake up. After a while I realized that she wasn't even there. I sat at the back of the house, drinking beer and putting the day's events into focus. I knew I'd end up killing someone if I stayed in Fort Qu'Appelle, and the thought of doing years or possibly life didn't sit well in my mind. I started walking down Main Street, toting my case of beer. I didn't see any police cars, or anyone else. I walked to the post office and sat on the lawn looking across the street at the lumberyard I'd robbed years ago. "I've got to hit the streets," I told myself. I lay down and thought of Devonne. I was going back to Regina as soon as I got some money together.

I woke up on the lawn in front of the post office, still holding a half-full beer. It was embarrassing, but it was six in the morning and only a few people saw me. I made plans quickly. I decided to contact Doug, my secret associate, in a way he wasn't expecting. I waited outside his house till dark, then I knocked on the front door.

"Well ... what the hell." His face was a mixture of fear and surprise. "When did you get out?"

"A few days ago. I got to talk to you." He shrugged and let me in. Doug was in his late thirties, and no match for me.

"What can I do for ..." He was cut off by my fist in his mouth. He went back over his glass coffee table. The table smashed, but before he could get his bearings I let him have a kick to the cheek bone. He reeled back against the couch. I grabbed the front of his shirt and pulled him toward me, letting him meet my other fist with his nose. Blood spurted over his furniture and clothes.

"Well Doug, long time no see."

"What do you want!"

"Don't shout, Doug. I'm right here. See, look at me." I grabbed him by the hair. "See, I'm right here. Don't yell or I'll knock you out and set your house on fire."

"What the hell did I do to you?" He was leaning against the couch, clutching his bleeding nose.

"I came for the money you owe me, Doug." I poured myself a scotch.

"What money!?"

"The money I let you take off me when I was gullible. Now it's payback." I smashed the bottle and held the jagged edge in front of his face. "Make your choice, Doug!"

"I've got no money!"

I back-handed him across the temple. "You've got more to lose than your money, Doug."

"Jim ..." He looked at me pleadingly. "I've only got a few hundred dollars. Please take that."

"Where is it?"

"In my wallet." He opened it up and pulled out $300. He handed it over with trembling hands. "This is it, Jim."

I grabbed the wallet. "Well, Dougie, you made an honest mistake, forgetting to look in your secret compartment. Let's see. Ah yes, 300 more." I stood up, counting the money. It totalled just under $700.

"Are you satisfied, Jim?" He gave me a disgusted look.

"Not really, Doug. What have you got to eat?" I looked in the kitchen.

"You said that's all you wanted!"

"I'll just take a look in the fridge, Doug, then I'll be on my way." There was some cold chicken from Gene's on a plate. I grabbed a couple of pieces and went back into the living room. Doug was studying me.

"You're not the same Jim I used to know."

"Times change, Dougie. People change. Things change. You know how it is." I finished the first piece of chicken and started on the second.

"Yeah, they do. But you shouldn't rob your friends. Hold up a gas station or something."

"Who said you were my friend?" I kept chewing.

"We did business in the past." His voice was thick with emotion. "I never screwed you around."

"You just took advantage of me by giving me dirt for the stuff I brought you. You consider yourself a fair man? Bullshit, Dougie!" I glared at him.

"Well ... you know how it is, Jim." His voice was more controlled.

I nodded. "That's why I robbed you." I got up and walked to the door. "See you."

I was back in Regina the next morning, and on the phone to Devonne. "Jimmy, so you're not back in jail yet." She giggled.

"What d'you say about a little breakfast?"

"Sure, Jimmy. You know where it is."

"I'll come over right away."

It was noon when Devonne and I sat at her kitchen table and I watched her getting ready for her octane boost. "How long have you been fixing?"

"Five, six years now." She smiled.

"How old are you?"

"You're not supposed to ask a lady that." She slapped me playfully on the forearm.

"What does tansi mean?"

"Tansi? How are you. Well Jimmy, how are you?"

"Fine now." We both laughed.

She looked at me for a moment. "Why would you ask me what tansi means? Don't you know how to speak Indian?"

"No. I'm from a white family and grew up with white people."

"Well, what do you know." She put her arms around me. "That's why you have no tattoos."

"Indians have tattoos?"

"Not all of them, but the ones on the street usually do. You don't know too many street people, do you?"

"Just the ones I met in jail."

"You must have seen a lot of guys with tattoos, then."

"I did, now that you mention it. But why do you figure growing up with white people explains me not having a tattoo?"

She lowered her eyes. "It's the way you act and talk. You sound smart, nice. You can tell you never came from a reserve, like most Indians. You grew up with more money in your family, right?"

"We were never starving," I replied nonchalantly.

"A lot of Indian people are starving — Indian children, because the rest of the family is drunk."

"Are you from ... one of those families?"

"I was." Her eyes bored into mine. "I ran to the city when I was

12, started pulling a few tricks, got raped three times by the time I was 15. Since then I always carry a knife. I've been stabbed three times, and I've stabbed people five times. That's my sob story, Tyman. What's yours?"

I was startled by her story. I turned my head to collect my thoughts about it. I hadn't seen her blink. "Does this happen a lot?"

"That's life on the street, Tyman. Survival of the fittest." She broke her expression to give me a faint smile.

"Well, I can't say I was raped three times, Devonne, because it only happened twice." I grinned broadly, and the tension broke. She was back to her playful laughter.

"What's it like growing up in a white family?"

"Oh it's ... it's different I would say, from reserve life." I shrugged. I didn't really know what it was like, except ... it was different.

"I know that, Jimmy. But what did they treat you like?"

"They treated me fine. But the racism was everywhere when I was growing up."

"Was your family racist?"

"Would they have adopted me if they were racist?"

"Probably not. But did you ever hear them make racist slurs or comments?"

I had to think about that. I'd heard them make a few. But then, didn't all white people? "Well yeah, kinda."

"Kinda, hey?" She gave me a suspicious look.

"Are you calling my family racists?"

"I'm saying they're a part of the white race, which is prejudiced against Indians. I was wondering if you became like that."

"You want to know if I was an apple, right?"

"Bingo. Did you ever get screwed up over your own identity type of thing?"

"Yeah, I did. How do you know about that type of thing?"

"I know a couple of girls downtown who were raised in white homes, and they said that white people were always trying to get them to change their identity, you know, just give up their heritage, and to attend church all the time, that type of shit. It fucked them up for a while. I was just wondering if you're like that."

I narrowed my eyes. "You're wondering if I'm a fuck-up?"

"Not a fuck-up fuck-up, Jimmy." She was trying to muffle her laughter. "But a ... an apple type of fuck-up."

"Oh, that type of fuck-up." I laughed with her. "Yeah, I guess you could say I was an apple. But what the hell, I must like Indians now," and I pinched her upper leg.

We spent the next two hours sharing memories, sharing a dream about getting rich and having no worries, and of course lots and lots of drugs. Devonne tried to give me a fix again. I declined, but ate two winnies instead. In half an hour I was floating, and Devonne was already on her second fix. "First time feels good, hey?" she asked. She poked the needle into her vein and pushed the plunger, then closed her eyes for a few seconds while the drug raced to her heart.

"Hey Devonne, you know where I can get some pot?" My voice was slow and low.

"No problem. How much?"

"Two ounces for sure, maybe three."

"You plan on selling some?"

"Yeah, then I can buy more with the profits."

"I'll be going out in a few hours. When I get back I'll let you know."

"Where do you work?"

"Downtown of course, anywhere. I ride alone usually. I got my own set of tricks, and they usually know where to find me once I get to a spot I like."

"I'll phone you tomorrow morning. How's that?"

"You're running away again, Jimmy!" she said quickly. "Why don't you stay? I'll bring back some booze and drugs and maybe a few good people and we'll have a party. You'll like some of the people I party with. You'll have a lot in common with each other."

"Former apples, right?"

"You got it." She laughed. "I'll phone you later tonight, then."

I walked around the house. It was nicely furnished. There was a cement basement where Barry kept his weight-lifting equipment. I never really thought Devonne was Barry's girl. She had said they were good friends and that they just helped each other out. Barry never talked much about her in jail. He just told me she was good people and that she wasn't his hooker, but she'd give him money if he asked for it, and vice versa. I wondered if this type of thing went on all over. I'd been led to believe that all hookers were controlled by a few pimps, but the way Devonne talked, it sounded like an open market, and hardly any one guy had more than two or three girls working for him. All you had to watch out for was working someone else's turf or taking another girl's trick, both of which could be hazardous to one's health.

I started looking through my crumpled bits of paper for addresses and phone numbers of former jail buddies. I phoned an Indian named Tony that I'd met in the fish range, but Tony had gone to Vancouver with his cousins who were drug runners. He'd got himself stabbed six times and more than likely lost the use of his right arm. He was 17.

I called another number, this time of a repeater I'd met in One D. He talked about setting up a drug business, since he had the connections in Winnipeg to buy lots of hashish. But he'd got out two weeks before me, and he was back in jail already for burglary.

I put on my coat and headed downtown to check out a few bars. I walked into the Lotus Hotel, which was known to cater to ex-cons and street people. I recognized half a dozen former convicts. I sat by the jukebox and ordered an Extra Old Stock beer from the overweight, overdressed waitress with dark blue eye shadow. She put on her sweetest smile and told me that she got off work at one if I wanted to stick around. I shook my head gently. She winked and walked to the next table. She whispered something to the guy there. He looked at her for a moment, gave her a big smile, and nodded. She had made her catch.

I sat in the Lotus for close to an hour, watching the street people. They were young and old. They were mostly Indians, but there were more white people than I'd anticipated. It made a difference which bar you were in. Some had a mix; others were Indian bars and the only white people were usually bartenders.

I decided to check out another bar. I went two blocks down the street to the Georgia Hotel, behind the Bay. I passed a couple of hookers on the way; Devonne wasn't one of them. I ordered my Extra Old Stock and listened to Stevie Nicks on the jukebox. I was feeling pretty good when in walked an ex-con. He was a white guy, but he was considered cool by other cons so I had no qualms about being associated with him. He recognized me right away and sat down.

"How's Tyman doing?"

"Not bad. What are you doing in this part of town?"

"Looking for some smoke. Do you know where I can find some?"

"You're from this town. Why're you asking me?"

"I've been in jail for the past year. You lose touch. Hey, why don't you come for a cruise? I've got a car outside."

"Sure, what the hell."

We walked through the parking lot to a shiny new Camaro.

"This is hot, right?"

"Come on, Tyman. You a woosie?"

Me? Weak-kneed and timid? I pointed a finger at him. "Don't even think of stopping if the pigs try to pull us over."

"Wouldn't cross my mind. This bitch could outrun those cop cars, anyway."

"We might find out," I answered quietly. I got in, making sure not to leave my prints on the door handle. We cruised Regina. We stopped at a few bars and a few nightclubs. We picked up a case of beer. It was twelve-thirty when my buddy decided to go to Saskatoon. "C'mon, Tyman. Let's check out the action up there. Maybe we'll get a couple of broads and come back this way. I know, if we don't like it we can go on to Edmonton. I've got a friend up there who'll put us up. By the way, where're you staying?"

I sighed. "Wherever I lay my head is home for the day."

"Me too. Great life, isn't it?"

"Yeah, it's freedom. I heard Tony got stabbed in Vancouver."

"Really? That's too bad. How did you hear about it?"

"I phoned his house and his sister told me."

"You should check out that bitch, Tyman. Man, I'll tell you she is one nice-looking woman. Too bad she's a hooker, though."

"Those are the best kind," I said. "At least they don't give it away like most broads do after two beers and a couple of joints."

He laughed. "You got a point there." He laughed louder, then banged the dash with the palm of his hand. "Sluts, all of them! Rotten sleaze-bags. Put them all on the street! Right, Tyman?"

"If they're willing."

"You going to get a bitch working for you?"

"I don't know. If they want."

"No, Tyman. Grab the bitch and make her work. That's the way you do it."

I thought of Devonne. "You figure that's the way to handle them? Beat them and dominate them?"

His voice rose with excitement. "Yeah! Beat, beat, beat them into a new understanding of the way it is!"

"That's not the way it is, pal."

"Sure it is. I know what goes on. I've been around, Tyman. I've been around."

I turned my head and sighed. Let him ramble on. Maybe that's the way it works for some people, but I wasn't going to do that. I was only going to beat, beat, beat the people who crossed me, not some girl who's had a tougher go of it than me. I started paying more attention to my case of beer and less attention to him.

We were about 50 miles from Saskatoon when my buddy came up with a suggestion. "Why don't we pull an AR while we're here. We won't even have to wear masks in this town. No one will know us. What d'you say?"

"I don't think that's a good idea."

"Sure it is. I've got a shotgun in the trunk, and look here." He reached under the seat and pulled out a seven-inch hunting knife. "Which do you want?"

I took the knife and ran my fingers over the blade. "What do you want to rob?"

"Anything that's open." He laughed. "I want to see the look on their face when they got a shotgun stuck in it."

I knew the guy was nuts, but I didn't know how to defuse this sudden passion for armed robbery. "I've got a few hundred bucks on me. We don't need that shit."

"You got that much? Whatcha do, rob an old man?" He laughed harder.

"I sold my ass." He stopped laughing and turned to look at me. "How much do you make in a night, Jim?" He was serious.

It was my turn to laugh. "I was juicing you. Look at me! Do I look like a male prostitute?"

He studied me for a minute. "Well no, I guess you aren't one of those. You're more a mugger type then a hooker type."

I told him to forget the armed robbery. He suggested robbing our way to Vancouver and down the coast to Los Angeles. "Think of it, Tyman. We could pick up girls along the way, buy lots of cocaine and booze. Let's do it." I kept trying to dissuade him, and he finally gave up the notion as we were coming under the overpass into Saskatoon. "Have you ever been to Saskatoon?"

"Never," I replied. I sat up and watched the street lights getting closer.

"I've only passed through on my way to Edmonton. But I hear it's a clean city, not like Regina."

"Yeah, I heard their jail is a real boys' center."

"I heard they give you your own key."

We cruised down Eighth Street. I thought it looked the same as Albert Street in Regina. My buddy was interested in something else.

"Where's all the hookers?" He demanded. He cranked up the radio. "Whoooh-weee! Let the good times roll!"

"Head to Twentieth Street." I suggested. I'd heard from guys in jail that that's where the street people hang out. We drove around for two hours before we realized we had to cross the river to find Twentieth Street. By that time we were driving in the morning sunshine. "I'm getting tired, man." He looked over at me. "Do you want to drive?"

"No problem." I'd been drinking beer all night. "Now we'll have fun."

"Don't get rank," he warned me.

"I won't pull any ARs while you're sleeping, anyway."

"You know what I mean. Don't get us arrested."

He pulled over by a park on the river. I pulled on his gloves so I wouldn't leave prints. The tires squealed as I pulled away from the curb. My friend protested faintly from the back seat, then he fell asleep. I drove down Twentieth Street. It was lined with bars in a three-block area. Actually, the whole downtown had bars everywhere. I was beginning to like the place already. I filled the tank at an all-night gas station and tipped the attendant $5.00. It was six o'clock in the morning when I spotted a police cruiser in the rear-view mirror. The Camaro was built for speed and sharp turns. I decided to test it. He was back about half a block. I put the accelerator to the floor, cranked the wheel, and went barrelling down a side street.

My friend bolted from sleep. "What's going on!"

"Just having a little fun." I cut down an alley. The cop overshot the turn and had to hit the brakes and back up. I stopped at the end of the alley.

"What are you doing!" His voice was filled with fear and excitement.

"Giving him a chance," I replied, and poured the rest of a beer down my throat.

"They've got radios, you know!" The veins in his neck were straining to get out from under his skin.

I roared away, making sure to leave a cloud of dust. I shot across the street into another alley. "Relax, pal. Hand me a beer."

"You're going to get us arrested, you bastard!" he shouted in my ear. But he handed me a beer.

I turned down a side street. We were between Twentieth Street and Twenty-Second. We skidded around corners, squealing the tires and raising dust. I just missed side-swiping a car. When we hit Twentieth again I drove right across and darted down the first alleyway I could find.

"I bet he went the wrong way when he came out of that dust," I laughed.

"You're nuts, Tyman!" He slumped back in the seat.

I raced onto the next street and turned away from Twentieth. I slowed down when we arrived on Seventeenth Street. I followed that to the river, then I followed the river until we were out in the country. I stopped the car to answer nature's call, and my friend was quick to jump into the driver's seat.

"Last time I let you drive."

"Whoooh-weee!" I yelled. "Let the good times roll!"

We drove through the country for two hours before we came to a highway. It ran right back to Twenty-Second Street. My friend was still upset and wouldn't talk to me till we rolled back into town. "I'm hungry. Why don't you buy me an egg and ham sandwich at McDonald's there." He pointed to the familiar giant yellow M.

"No problem, if you let me drive this baby again."

"No way, man!"

"Well ..." I used my best soothing voice. "I could get us lots of food and booze and drugs, and maybe a couple of women, if I was behind the wheel of this sports car. You know they like a big strong man behind a big strong car. If things go right, we could spend the night" — I looked around for a motel — "there. Look, it's got waterbeds!" I let him hear the excitement in my voice. "It's got cable, too! And look, there's a pizza joint right there! There's even a liquor store across the street! We got it made! We might even stay for a while!" I lowered my voice and slumped in the passenger's seat. "But you want to drive ... and be spiteful."

"You're an asshole, Tyman!" he shot back, then added softly, "but you can drive."

We made the exchange in the parking lot. I bought him two Egg McMuffins with ham, while I had another Extra Old Stock. I drove around for a while, taking it fairly easy, until my friend demanded I get us a room. I headed back to the motel on Twenty-Second Street.

I parked the car in a lot down the street. At the motel I rented one room with two single beds under the name of Johnny Longfeather, with my brother Joey. I lay down and watched Saturday morning cartoons while my friend started snoring on the next bed. I was waiting for eleven o'clock when I could walk across the street and get some more beer. I thought of phoning Devonne. I wondered if another Jimmy Tyman had come home with her last night.

I thought about my options. I could probably live all right if I stayed with Devonne in Regina. I thought of going somewhere else — Edmonton, Vancouver, maybe Toronto. I'd heard stories about Toronto and Yonge Street and all the money that could be made there. Cons always talked about other cities and the romping good times they'd had there. I wanted some of that, but I was also looking for a sense of security like Devonne had. She had a nicely furnished place, the bills were paid, there was food in the house. I wanted that stability. My sleeping friend reminded me of the cons who wanted to go like gangbusters till they got caught or killed. I didn't want that.

I lay there more tired than drunk, waiting patiently till eleven. At ten-thirty I decided to walk across the street and check out the Westgate Mall. There wasn't much to it. An OK Economy store was the biggest attraction. There was a large clothing store at the other end, and in between there was a bank, a restaurant, and various boutiques. I was standing outside the liquor store when I looked across the street and saw a police car at the motel. It drove around slowly, then stopped in front of our room. I was wide awake and sober now. Two uniformed officers jumped out of the cruiser and started walking toward our door. I was planning my escape back to Regina when they knocked on the next door. They banged for five minutes before a disgruntled, middle-aged man opened the door. They went inside, emerging 10 minutes later with the man looking more shaken than disgruntled. He got in the back of the police car and it roared away. I started feeling drunk and tired again.

I was back in the motel room with a case of beer and a bottle of whisky, watching a ball game on TV. I had half the beer drunk before my buddy rolled over and opened his eyes.

"What time is it?"

"Around three o'clock." I jumped off the bed. "C'mon, let's go cruising."

"Where to?"

"Downtown, where else?"

"Let's get something to eat first."

"Okay, I'll get you a Ronnie Raunch burger. But let's get rolling. I want to see the people."

Later, we were sitting in the Albany Hotel. My buddy was drinking with me this time, and he started getting rowdy. "C'mon, Tyman! Let's kick some ass!"

"Wait for trouble," I said. "Don't cause it."

He spotted someone he was sure he could handle. I wasn't watching him closely enough. Before I knew it he'd got up and proceeded to punch the bewildered guy in the face. I turned at the sound of the screams and curses. The bouncer and I got there at the same time. We separated them, and my buddy started taunting the other guy. He was pumped.

"You two are barred!" the bouncer shouted.

"Fuck you, asshole!"

The bouncer went for him, but I blocked him with a right

cross to the temple which sent him tumbling across a table, spilling more drinks. My buddy seized the opportunity to smash his opponent in the mouth. He crumpled to the floor, unconscious. The bouncer got up and started for me. My buddy smashed a beer bottle and egged him on — "C'mon, you woosie!" — all the time faking stabs with the jagged edge of the bottle.

"You guys just get the hell out of here!" the bartender shouted from behind the bouncer.

I knew this was the time to vacate the premises; the cops had been phoned. With my buddy holding the bottle on them we backed out the door. We went for the car just as the police were rounding the corner. We roared away — two blocks down and into the Windsor Hotel. Bad mistake.

I was telling my buddy to be cool and try and have a good time. "Wait for trouble to start, pal. Then we'll kick some ass, okay?"

"Yeah, yeah!" His voice was high and excited. "We'll show these bastards that Regina is number one, yeah!"

Everything started well. I was talking to a couple of girls who were asking me all types of personal questions. I was obliging with tales of the days when I used to ride in the rodeo. They gobbled it up. Then I told them how I was a miner from up north and I was just looking for a little loving before I had to go back into that deep dark hole, maybe never to come back. They were moved and offered their assistance. I was getting up to tell my buddy about our good fortune when I saw the shine of his blade slicing through the air. He must have taken it from under the seat of the car when I wasn't looking.

"What d'you think of that!" His distinctive voice screeched over the noises of alarm and horror. The victim was clutching his chest. He had a 12 inch slash starting at his left shoulder and cutting down at a 45 degree angle. I reacted quickly. I grabbed my buddy and raced out the door. He was taunting other people, challenging them to come and play outside. We made it to the car and were out of the parking lot just as the ambulance and the police arrived.

I looked over at my buddy, who was wiping the blade of the knife. "Last time I buy you a drink!" I commented.

He looked at me for a minute, then gave me a half smile. "Whoooh-weee! Let the good times roll!"

I couldn't help myself. I started laughing with him. I didn't stop till we were 60 miles out of town on the road back to Regina. We were going home to wherever we laid our heads.

* * *

We rolled back into the city about one o'clock. I pulled into the McDonald's drive-through on Albert Street to buy my annoying buddy a hamburger and fries. Then I took him to Devonne's. Another mistake. She had a few friends over, but I was glad to see she wasn't taken for the night. She smiled broadly. "Well, well. Where has the hoodlum been? And who's your friend?"

"Joey Longfeather, my brother."

"He's not your brother." She punched me playfully. "Who is he?"

"A friend from jail."

"Hello, friend from jail. I'm Devonne."

"Pleased to meet you." He smiled. "Jim here tells me lots about you."

She shot a glance at me. "Like what?" It was more a demand than a question.

He smiled and looked around the room. "That you're a good lay."

Devonne stormed out of the room. I knew where she was going. She had her own seven-inch hunting knife.

"You asshole!"

"She's just a hooker."

There were three other hookers and their old men in the room when he chose to make this casual observation. One guy jumped up, then Devonne came out with her knife raised high. My buddy reached for his.

"Cool it!" I grabbed his arm and stepped in front of him, blocking Devonne.

"Out of the way, Tyman!" She hissed. "I'll shank that bastard!"

"He's leaving, Devonne. I'm sorry he's like that, but I'll get him out of here. Don't waste your time with him. He's gone." I waited a century while Devonne mulled it over. The other people waited on their toes, ready to spring.

"Well, get him out of here then!" She pointed to the door with her knife. "If I ever see you again, you bastard, I'll cut you up so bad you'll never have kids!" She meant every word.

I pushed him out the door, blocking with my body to prevent anyone from shanking him in the back. When I got him outside I told him thanks for the lovely comment, and floored him with a right uppercut. I walked back inside telling myself the guy was just plain lucky. Devonne was still steamed. She told me if I ever brought over another asshole like that, I'd be the one getting shanked, in my sleep if necessary.

Later I sat at the kitchen table with Devonne and a few people. There was a prostitute named Diana who was my age, 19 or so. Devonne said we should get to know each other, considering we'd both been apples at one time. Diana was from Yorkton, but after constant run-ins with her foster parents, her school, and the white population, she packed her belongings in a duffel bag, jumped on a bus, and headed for Vancouver. She stopped in Regina to see a cousin and ended up staying. She'd been working the streets ever since.

Calvin was a guy in his late fifties, with graying hair. He told me I had a promising future on the street. He was considering my looks and size. "You'll have hordes of women, Jimmy." He smiled like a father. "I wish I was your age again. Damn, if I was you, there's no telling what I could have done."

Rob was a pimp about 25. He had a slim build and hard-looking eyes. He wasn't as impressed with me as Calvin was. He was more concerned with where I'd met that asshole than whether I'd have a harem by his age. Jealousy is a good enough reason to die when you're on the street.

I was again offered the needle. When there are six people staring at you who fix as a regular pastime, it's not easy to say no. Calvin understood when I told him I'd never fixed before. He started reminiscing about the first time he shot up as he crushed the two winnies and added the hot water and started to stir them up in the spoon. He used a clean cigarette filter to strain the liquid so the needle wouldn't clog. Then he found a vein and squeezed the works into my forearm.

I felt the ether engulf my air passages. I broke into a sweat. I struggled with my stomach. It was erupting with the rush from the drug. I struggled to keep my head up and my eyes open. I felt like getting sick. I thought I was going to pass out. One thing I did notice was that the other people in the room had visibly relaxed. I was one of them now, not an intruder but a fellow hype.

I sat at the table with Calvin, who briefed me about life on the street. He told me how to handle a beef, who was who, who thought they were who, and who to watch out for. Street people were basically living off life's vices, he said: prostitution and drug trafficking, with a few armed robberies and thefts thrown in to make ends meet. I listened like a small child. After an hour he offered me another fix. I accepted, to the obvious approval of the party. This time I had to puke. I made it to the bathroom just in time to let my guts explode into the toilet. When I got back to the table I felt a whole lot better. My friend told me that when you throw up you actually get higher. "You should have puked the first time, Jimmy," and he erupted in laughter. All the time I'd thought I was being cool by holding my guts inside.

The next morning I was still alive — surprisingly, considering I'd shot up four times during the night, I hadn't slept in 48 hours, and I'd consumed a barrel of beer and a bottle of whisky. Calvin wanted to get some more booze and winnies. I offered to pay for everything. I could hardly walk, but he went steady and sure to his car. He told me how glad he was to meet me, that I was good people, and once again how he wished he was my age.

As we drove to the pusher's and then to the bootlegger's, I was wondering why people hated Indians so much. All last night, this guy had never once bad-mouthed white people. Whenever the subject came up, he just said that white people generally have been influenced into hating Indian people. "I know a lot of honkies, Jimmy," Calvin had said. "They aren't all bad. It's the society we live in that makes them that way. They have a lack of understanding toward Indian people and their ways." He smiled broadly, then added, "But I think you know what I mean, eh apple?" I turned red- faced and everyone had a hearty laugh.

My generosity cost me $120. We purchased four cases of beer and another dozen winnies. Calvin said he got a deal for them, but I didn't know how much they were in the first place. We got back to Devonne's about nine in the morning. There were only three people up. The rest were on the couch, the floor, in the spare bedroom. Devonne was wasted. She asked me my name twice.

We sat at the table once again as Calvin crushed up six winnies. Then he and Devonne and myself all had our fix. It caused me to throw up again. It finished Devonne. She stood up and weaved around, then crashed in an arm chair. I stumbled back to the table, refusing to go under. I started drinking beer and talking away about anything. Calvin nodded with glassy eyes as he prepared another shot. Rob came over and had a fix and grabbed a couple of beers and made his way back to the couch where his old lady lay naked under the blanket.

I awoke on the floor clutching a beer. It was dark outside. Devonne was cleaning up the bottles. I couldn't remember when I'd gone under. My head was sore. So was my forearm; there was a large bruise where Calvin had missed my vein.

"What time is it?" My voice was raw and dry.

"Ten-thirty."

I rolled onto my side. "Where did everyone go?"

"Home sweet home, I guess." She glanced toward me. That's

when I saw the welt under her left eye.

I got up quickly. "What happened to you?"

"Rob hit me. I wouldn't lend him any money." She was more disgusted than hurt.

"Why does he want money? What's wrong with his woman?" The welt was about a quarter-inch high. Rob had obviously been wearing a ring; the imprint was visible on her swollen skin.

"I don't know. He always acts that way when he's drunk." She could see the tension building in my face. "Don't worry about it, Jimmy. He'll come and apologize like he always does."

"Look, Devonne. I know I'm not your old man or anything, but if Barry was here he wouldn't have done anything like that. And Barry is my friend, so ..." My voice trailed off.

She had a quizzical look on her face. "Are you trying to tell me you'll look after this?"

"Yeah, I guess I am."

"Do you want me to work for you?"

"If you want. But don't think this is my way of making you think you have to. You don't have to. I can get by. I'll just rob old people and stuff like that."

She was smiling. "What about your granny?"

"Oh, I'll cut her in when she needs help." We both laughed.

I was downtown the next night. I ran into Calvin in the bar. I told him what had happened and what I was planning to do. He told me to be careful; Rob carried a knife.

"Would you be doing this, Calvin?" I needed some reassurance.

He looked at me with his passive, gentle face. "Yes I would, if I were you. It was wrong what he did, but it's none of my business. If you want to make it your business, then that's exactly what it is." He gave me a nod of approval, and I left with a fresh hit of adrenalin running through my veins.

I was heading for a hotel by the police station — the hotel has burnt down since then — when who should I see walking my way but Rob. I stared at him hard. He tensed immediately.

"Why are you gunning me off, Tyman?"

"Because you're an asshole." I smiled at him.

He took a swing with his right. I ducked and brought up my own fist into his ribs. I heard them crack. He let out a gasp and backed away, clutching his side.

"Rob, can I borrow some money?"

"Fuck you, Tyman! I'll get my brothers after you."

"In that case, let's make it worthwhile."

I kicked him in the face. He fell onto his back. I grabbed him by the hair and let him have a series of straight rights until his face was a mask of blood. He was unconscious, but I kept hitting him. I was suspended in a time warp. The blare of a car horn snapped me out of it. The car stopped. I raced over to it. I was still pumped, and the driver didn't have much doubt that he'd made a mistake, trying to act the good Samaritan. He started to drive away. I managed to put my boot to his back fender, then I went back to Rob. I could tell his nose was shattered—not broken, but literally shattered. His eyes would be closed for two weeks. His bottom lip was hanging like a piece of shredded meat. His top lip was split in two places. I couldn't tell if I'd knocked out any of his teeth; there was too much blood to see. I turned him on his side. I didn't want him to choke to death on his own blood.

I looked down the street. There were three hookers watching, but they knew the code of the street. You stay silent if you want to go on living healthy and carefree. I walked to the bar by the police station and cleaned up my hands. People looked at me suspiciously as I walked through and into the bathroom with blood dripping down my fingers. My right hand was swollen. The knuckles were intact but very bruised, or possibly cracked. I'd cracked them three times already on people's faces. It was the way I grew up: fight them or submit to them. I didn't submit to them.

I came out of the bathroom to see one of the hookers from the street talking to this guy who was a hell of a lot bigger than me.

"Hey, you!" His eyes said what he wanted to do to me. "You fuckin' asshole!"

"Are you talking to me, pal?"

"Yeah, I'm talking to you. That was my friend!" He came toward me.

I knew what he was about to do, and all I can say is, I'm glad I was sober. I let him get closer. I moved my hands quickly, and when I saw his eyes focus on them, I booted him with all my might square in the balls. He bent over, and I kicked him in the face. He fell back clutching his testicles while blood began flowing out of his mouth. I took the opportunity to vacate the premises. I wasn't going to stick around to see if this guy had friends.

The prostitute who had caused this latest altercation stood nervously outside. I nodded like a true gentleman. "Nice evening for a walk, ma'am."

She had one hand in her purse, probably clutching a knife. "Who are you?"

"My name is Adam, ma'am. Adam Apple." I turned and walked away.

Two days later, with Devonne's help, I purchased four ounces of Mexican Red Hair. I was off and about daily, in the bars, the malls, peddling my dope. I did well, and soon bought four more ounces. Devonne's eye healed well enough for her to get back on the street, which made her happy. She wanted money to buy her drugs of choice. She was strictly a narcotics gal, and only occasionally smoked grass.

Word was filtering back to her about some big Indian named Adam Apple who had beat up Rob. The word also said that Rob required over 50 stitches to repair his lips, and 20 more for two serious cuts below his eyes. His nose was shattered, and plastic surgery seemed to be in order.

"You messed him up real bad, Jimmy," she said, with a touch of gratitude.

"I'm sorry, Devonne. It was Adam Apple who did it." I

shrugged. "I can't take credit for another man's accomplishments."

She smiled, and hugged me. "Well okay, if that's the way it is, Tyman." She giggled. "I mean Adam."

I was walking through the Cornwall Center when I got a spontaneous urge to go back to Saskatoon. I picked up a bottle of whisky for the two-and-a-half-hour bus ride, and sat in the back of the Greyhound watching the countryside fade in the sunset. I sipped from the bottle and pondered what to do when I got there. Saskatoon offered new horizons and people, and in the back of my mind I was thinking I might find some Martins in the city. My real beginning was always on my mind.

I got off the bus just after ten o'clock at night and headed for the strip with my bottle of whisky tucked under my jacket. I went into different bars this time. There are lots to choose from in downtown Saskatoon, so finding a good bar wasn't the problem. The problem was trying to get to every one of them before closing.

It was near one-thirty when I found myself in a situation I hadn't considered before: I had no place to go. I scanned the bar quickly. I was looking for a girl who looked lonely or a group of people heading for a party. There were no young girls available, and the groups were nothing but the older crowd, probably heading for the one-room flats above the businesses that lined Twentieth Street. Not my crowd at all.

I walked out with a 12 pack, considering my options. I could rent a room, or I could sit in the park by the river and proceed to get drunker. I chose the latter. I was two blocks away when from out of a dark shadow emerged an older Indian, about 40 years old. "Hey bro, grab some. Let's go." He had two full cases of beer, plus one that had four or five bottles left. I grabbed some and we went.

We got to the park in the early morning hours, about half past two. Within minutes we were laughing and joking like long-lost friends. There was a dock for tour-boat passengers jutting into the river. We sat on it with our pant legs rolled up and our feet in the water, guzzling beer and tossing the empties into the river. We drank the better part of the night away before I finally got around to asking the man's name.

"Randy. Randy Crow is my name. What's your name, bro?"

"Jim Tyman."

"Well, Jim Tyman, I'm heading up north to do some fishing this weekend. Why don't you come with me?"

"Where up north?"

"Way up north." He waved expansively toward the south. I guess we were pretty drunk. "We'll go up past La Ronge, past the Churchill."

"Do you know where Ile-à-la-Crosse is?"

"Of course I do. I lived there for five years."

I felt a bit of excitement. "Do you know any Martins up there?"

"Hell, yeah." His voice boomed over the still South Saskatchewan River. "There's lots of them boys up there."

Now I wanted to go with him. "How many?"

"Well, let me see." He paused to contemplate. "I'd say at least 20. They're not all from the same family, but they're all related one way or another. They're all half French, too. Actually, that whole town is Métis."

I was mulling over these facts when Randy Crow filled me in on more interesting details: "A couple of Martins from up there live right here in town. They drink down at the Baldwin Hotel. Ask around. You're sure to run into one of them."

I looked at him closely. He wasn't joking. But then, why would he? He didn't know what had been on my mind all my life.

As the sun rose a park crew came by, spraying for mosquitoes. Without warning, Randy lay down and passed out. I moved to one of the park benches and drank beer while morning joggers passed. It didn't take long to decide I was going to move to Saskatoon.

I was dead tired by eleven o'clock when I wandered into the Baldwin for an eye-opener. I'd bought a local paper and started to look over the classifieds for apartments around town. They ranged from $100 to $500. I wasn't choosy. I circled a one-room apartment just down the street. That's where I wanted to live, downtown near the strip, near the action.

I left the bar with an urge to play pinball. It was one of my favorite pastimes, and still is. I spotted Duck's Arcade on Third Avenue, and walked in to find a horde of teenagers. I knew from the atmosphere that this was the bad kids' hangout. There were obviously drugs in use at the back table. The teenagers were dressed in black leather from head to foot. Their hair was long and ragged. Their mouths were foul and offensive. They were my type of people.

I spotted a young Indian girl who smiled briefly in my direction. She was seated with some friends who were chewing gum defiantly. I turned away, but I was compelled to keep looking back at her. She went to a video game and started to play. I walked up to her and watched her guide the Pac-Man through the maze. "How're you doing?" I asked.

She gave me another quick smile, but she didn't answer. "Do you come around here a lot?" I pressed.

"Yeah, most of the time."

I nodded and smiled. "You going out partying tonight?"

"Probably."

I was still smiling and nodding. "Do you smoke grass?"

She didn't answer for a minute. She wasn't smiling. She was studying me and making a decision. "Yeah, I like to smoke grass. You got some?"

"Well, of course." I smiled broadly.

"That's nice."

I studied her. She sure was pretty. She looked about 16, 17. "I'll give you a toke. What d'you say?"

"Sure thing." She smiled sweetly, and showed me to a back door in the arcade. I produced the joint of Red Hair. We stood between two buildings and smoked it. "Do you want to go to the bar and have a few beer?"

"I can't tonight. My friends and I are going to a party up in

Fairhaven." She paused for a moment to study me. "Maybe next time."

I nodded. I wanted to ask her where Fairhaven was. I didn't know it was a neighborhood of Saskatoon.

We went back inside and she sat with her friends. I hung around and played a couple of games. As I walked out I glanced back in her direction. She was still busy talking to her friends. I left kicking myself for not being able to bring her along with me.

The apartment building was two blocks off Twentieth Street. It was a former office building which had been renovated for low-income housing. It was obvious there would be no problem getting an apartment here. Indians were coming and going when the grizzled old landlord showed me the one-room apartment. It was only twice as big as my jail cell, but it had a fridge and stove and kitchen table, plus a single bed. I handed over a month's rent. I had a home.

I went bar hopping down Twentieth Street with the last of my money, around $50. I watched the street people of Saskatoon. They were mostly natives, and they seemed no different from Regina's—prostitutes, pimps, pushers, as well as the pathetic and the perverse. I sat at different tables. Everyone I sat with was as drunk as I was, and no one ever remembered who had invited who to sit down. I stuck out because of my size. And I was the new guy on the scene. The local pimps were studying me. I paid no attention to them, just their girls, who would smile quickly when their pimps weren't looking.

I started to ask a few people if they knew any Martins. It became apparent that there were lots of them around. "Which one? There's lots of them in town, Jim." Then I remembered what Randy Crow had said about the ones that hung around downtown, and I narrowed it down to half a dozen possibilities. There were Martins right in the bar. They were sitting with the prostitutes and pimps. I looked at the three my buddy pointed to. They didn't look like me at all. I tried to narrow it down more.

"Do you know if they're from Ile-à-la-Crosse?"

"That one is for sure." He pointed to the clean-cut one. He was in his thirties, and bore no resemblance to me at all.

I studied him. I wanted to go up and ask him if he knew ... if he knew what? What could I say? "Hi, my name is Kenny. Remember me?" He'd probably look at me like I was some man dressed in bed sheets toting a Bible and asking for money. It wasn't a good idea. I decided just to watch him and get more information by casual conversation.

It was obvious the guy was a pimp. I wondered what the hell had led him to that. Then I thought of myself, and what had led me to be sitting in a bar full of pimps and prostitutes. I shook my head and ordered another Extra Old Stock.

By last call I was feeling down and out. I remembered when the in crowd used to ask about my real family, I could always get a few laughs by saying they were probably a bunch of pimps and prostitutes now.

I turned down invitations to parties and sat silently as the bar emptied. I gathered my last bills and purchased a case of beer and walked out the back door, heading for my one-room home. I sat by the window overlooking the street. There were a few prostitutes still out. I watched as the same car went round and round the block till finally the driver got enough nerve to stop. I watched the scene and sipped my beer, trying to put my thoughts into focus. There wasn't much to focus on. If I hadn't been adopted I would probably have ended up here anyway, in this dingy apartment building, partying with street people, living with whores, shooting dope in my arm, not knowing what direction to take in my life.

My need for money overcame my thoughts of what might have been. I grabbed a couple of beers and headed for the street, looking for an easy score. It didn't take long. The area was littered with businesses. The burglary was quick and to the point. I saw leather coats and a ghetto blaster in the store, and I knew both articles would sell quickly on the street.

I spent the next couple of days selling the goods and partying. The parties were all the same. I'd meet a girl in the bar, and after the formalities I'd be going home with her, or to some private get-together. I met a lot of street people this way. That first week in Saskatoon I spent only one night at my place, which was just as well. I didn't have a sheet or a blanket to cover myself at night, and the mornings were pure hell. There were no curtains and no air conditioning, and on a June morning the sun shining through the large south window would swell the temperature into the high eighties by noon. There was a community bathroom on each floor, used by up to 15 people daily. Only a select few cleaned up after themselves, so the smell of human waste was dominant in the shadowy hallways. I wouldn't tell street people where I lived. This complex was below the standards of most of them.

There were some young people on my floor, but after I drank with them one night it became apparent where they were headed. They spent half an hour explaining the fine art of mixing Lysol with water or Coca-Cola, or the beauty of drinking vanilla extract with milk. "It tastes good on a hot day, Jim." Then one night I came home to find them walking by with my radio and the few groceries I had in the fridge. Their door was locked when I went to confront them, so after five minutes of hammering on it I just booted it down. There, like three children crowded behind the bed, sat my neighbors. I grabbed the first guy, who started to whine that he was sorry and it wasn't his idea. I looked at him. He was pathetic, sweaty and greasy, only 20 years old. I let him have a blow behind the ear. It knocked him to the floor, where he lay whimpering. The other two, a man and a woman, stood wide-eyed behind the bed. Finally the woman went into a tirade at me for booting the door down and how I was going to get them thrown out of the apartment. I pointed to the window and asked her if she wanted to go out tonight. She shook her head silently.

They were pathetic. I could see the self-pity in their faces, in the sunken eyes, the slumped shoulders. They were no one's creatures. People didn't want them in their apartment buildings. No one wanted to be seen with them on the street. They had a circle of friends who looked the same or worse, who spent the hot summer nights drinking vanilla extract mixed with cool milk on the fire escape at the back of the building. These thoughts took the steam out of my anger. I told them just to give me back my stuff and I'd be out of there. As I was leaving, the whimpering of the man on the floor got to me, and I threw them a package of sausages. At least they'd have something to eat tonight.

I was sitting in a bar by myself once again when along came the young girl I had seen in the arcade. She was looking fine. She was with a prostitute I had seen on the street. I concluded she was a whore herself. She saw me at the table and sat down, all smiles. I asked her if she wanted a beer. She accepted, then she told me she was only 15. I thought she was lying, then she showed me her ID. It was true. She was born in December 1967. But she could pass for 19 easily. The waitress knew her by name and asked her what she was up to. Then she asked me for ID!

We sat and talked about anything. She was damn good looking, but she was only 15. I wasn't going to run around with girls under 16. It was bad luck. It was also illegal. It was statutory rape. In jail you were a skinner, the worst scum in sight. If you were murdered or beaten for being a skinner, the other inmates cheered. I was going to avoid that at all costs, even though going out with her seemed so right. She was so pretty, and so sweet.

Her name was Donna Nighttraveller. She had been around the street for the past year. She enjoyed partying with street people. They were good people, she said, except for the rank ones who ruined a party by knifing someone. I agreed with her. A knifing can really put a damper on the festivities.

I was getting drunk with her, so the thought of at least partying with her didn't seem all wrong. We went to the hotels down Twentieth. She knew quite a few people also, including the man I thought might be my brother. We bought two hits of acid off a local dealer who was sitting with him. I asked her if she knew him, and she said he was her uncle. I slumped back in my chair. I had wanted to go out with my own niece!

"What's wrong with you?"

"Nothing at all. Let's go to another bar, one with rock n' roll. You like rock and roll, don't you?" Most Indian people were into country music.

"Right on. There's rock and roll just down the street at Sneakies. It's open till five so you can party all night." She was getting off on the acid and laughed spontaneously. I kept wondering if she was my niece.

"You ever been to Ile-à-la-Crosse?"

"Yeah, lots of times. It's nice up there, Jim. Are you thinking of going?"

"Yeah. D'you wanna come?"

She looked at me for a moment. "I'll think about it."

I grumbled to myself and took a swallow of beer. I had just asked my niece for a date.

As it turned out, we didn't get into the bar because of her age. I guess not everyone knew who she was. We bought a case of beer and went to an arcade in the same building. I met a few of her friends. They were all about the same age. I did my best to be courteous, but I was more interested in drinking in a bar. At the same time I didn't want to leave Donna's side. She fascinated me. Could she be my niece? She was obviously a hooker.

I didn't know what to expect when I found my real family, but this was not it. I was hoping for something else, obviously — a family gathering, everyone hugging me, tears flowing, a lost childhood explained. Pimps and prostitutes were not what I was expecting. But then, where was I now? "Fuck it," I told myself, as I'd told myself a thousand times before. "Let the good times roll!" Drink hard and forget the pain. That was the way to go. It was everyone's way down Twentieth.

After meeting her friends in the arcade we went outside and drank beer in the alley. We talked about everything. I learned of her upbringing, about life on the reserve near North Battleford. Poverty was the norm. There was no running water in most households. That shocked me. Didn't every household in Canada have running water? She went on about the filth and the disease. If you stayed on the reserve there was simply nothing for you — no money, no jobs, just open space and loads of time to drink and fight. She went on about incidents of violence, how one old man used to take shots at you with his rifle if you went across his land. Then there was the bad medicine lady who put spells on you if you didn't submit to her demands. Donna's older brother was very sick once, she said, and suffering temporary blindness. Then their mother went to the good medicine woman on the reserve to get the bad spells lifted, and he recovered within a week. This took place because their mother and the bad medicine woman had had an argument over Indian and white relationships. Their mother supported a better understanding between the two races, while the medicine lady preferred another Indian war to wipe out all the honkies.

I didn't believe her at first. It seemed a bit far-fetched. But why would she lie? It made me relax a little, anyway, knowing she wasn't from Ile-à-la-Crosse. Now I didn't believe she was my niece. But then, if she wasn't my niece, then her uncle wasn't my brother. I was back to square one.

Two days later I walked into Duck's Arcade where I'd first seen her. She was with a friend I hadn't met. They were both dressed mighty fine. I was drunk, and walked up to her and asked point blank if she was going out to pull tricks for the night. She slapped my face hard, and was going for a second one when I stopped her. I apologized humbly. She accepted, warning me not to accuse her of such a thing ever again. I never did.

I went back to Regina to retrieve my clothes. It was only a suitcase full. Devonne was disappointed and upset. As I left her house she told me that there were other Jimmy Tymans around, and that I blew it. I waved to her and thanked her for the good times. She gave me the finger. I shrugged and motioned to the cab driver to take me to the bus depot and back to Saskatoon.

I saw Donna Nighttraveller only once in a while for the next few months. By July of that year I had struck up a relationship with a woman in her early thirties, and I was living with her. She was constantly being asked for her ID in bars, and her face beamed with the compliment the waitresses didn't realize they were making. She was a country singer, and performed at bars and dances. Our relationship was brief. She was an alcoholic, and her personality would make a complete turnaround once the booze was in her. On one occasion I tried to stop her from booting a friend of hers in the head. The friend lay passed out on the floor. She went for the knives she kept tucked under her mattress. I didn't know about them until she raced out of the bedroom. I ducked the first thrust, but the second one caught me below the ear, just missing the artery in my neck. I knocked her to the floor, and she started crying like a baby. As I was leaving she jumped on my back, screaming that I couldn't leave and asking why I didn't love her. She had made plans for my future. She was well off. She lived in a nice building with satellite TV, a whirlpool, sauna, weight room, tennis courts, a pool. The apartment had all the latest accessories, and I was being seduced by the thought of living in luxury. She promised to bring home the bacon. All I had to do was supply my manhood. But after a near-fatal knife wound, I wanted no part of my country singer any more.

I started bouncing in the bar of the Continental Hotel on Twentieth Street. I was supposed to break up fights now instead of start them. The job was good for one thing: I met another woman who wanted to look after me. But this time instead of succumbing to her desires I played up to them, and was promptly given a place to live and food to eat. If I would sit and listen and seem genuinely concerned about her for a night, then she was happy. She was like everyone I met on the street: lonely, and wanting a little love and understanding. Filling that role filled my own needs on occasion. She was married, so I called her the adulteress, though she wasn't living with her husband any more.

I met a friend at the hotel where I was bouncing. Brian was my age, a cheerful and happy-go-lucky type of guy. We'd party up a storm down the strip every night when we had money. I stayed with him and his girlfriend some nights. They had an apartment about 15 blocks up Twentieth. Other nights I stayed with a girl I met at the bar, or at the adulteress's house when I knew she'd found a man for the night and I could be sure of being left alone. Home was wherever I lay my head in the summer of '83.

I quit my job one night. I'd been threatened by a local pimp who didn't like the smiles I gave to his girls. He told the bartender I was dead unless I quit. I was told and agreed to quit. It was affecting my health, and I didn't really give a damn when they fought themselves. Besides, the pimp was the man who might have been my brother. I didn't want to die at his hands, and I didn't want to have to kill him in self-defense either.

It was August. I'd been staying with Brian and his girlfriend, Sandy. We'd been holed up in their apartment for three days, boozing, smoking, and occasionally fighting. At twelve-thirty on the last night of our booze and drug fest, we pooled our money for one last case of beer. I was called upon to ride Brian's bike down to the bar to get it. His bike was in a rack with a dozen others from the same apartment complex. Being drunk and impatient, I grabbed the first bike I could pry loose from the pile. It was a three-speed girl's model. Unfortunately, the owner saw me take it and promptly told her father, who promptly phoned the police. I hadn't gone five blocks when the cruiser pulled me over.

"Out for a little bike ride, are we?" The young blonde officer threw me to my stomach by the side of the road.

"Take it easy, pal. It ain't murder," I shot back over my shoulder while I heard an old tune playing: the locking of handcuffs on my wrists.

I was formally charged with theft under $200 for stealing a three-speed Classic, valued at $45, bought at a garage sale the previous day. Things weren't over, though. Fort Qu'Appelle had dug up a two-year-old warrant for open liquor in a public place. It was a $25 ticket, but somehow when I was going up for parole it never came across on the crime index report. Some tenacious officer had spent the time going over the files to find my unpaid infraction. I was given a promise to appear to be back in Fort Qu'Appelle in a week, to have a judge — the same judge who had sentenced me to prison — set the new fine and the conditions of payment. I was to be back in Saskatoon in two weeks to answer to the charge of theft under $200. Considering my record, I'd probably get 30 days for stealing that damn bike. I should have had more patience that night.

* * *

It was on the bus to Fort Qu'Appelle the following week that I decided to head for Vancouver as soon as I could round up enough money for a train ticket. The train had a bar car; it wouldn't be like a long, dry bus trip. I'd head down to Los Angeles after a brief stay in Vancouver.

I walked into court in Fort Qu'Appelle vowing this would be the last time I would been seen in this town.

"Why haven't you paid this ticket?" the judge demanded.

"I forgot about it."

"Do you have a memory problem also?"

"No."

"In that case, I'll raise the ticket fine to $120. Do you have the money?"

"Not $120. I have the $25, though."

"That's too bad. Do the time. Thirty days." He motioned to a surprised police officer to take an even more surprised me away.

"What's that guy's problem?" I asked.

"Tired of seeing the same faces." He smiled broadly.

I sat in the same cells that I'd visited at least 30 times before. I was waiting to go back to the Regina Correctional Center. There were three young Indians, 16 to 18 years old, waiting along with me. It was their first time, and they peppered me with questions.

"Is it pretty rank?"

"It has its moments."

"Lot of drugs inside?" This kid was born fixing; he was a talking brown skeleton.

"Yeah, there's lot's of dope floating around."

I sat there for 30 minutes before a cop came back to tell me I had a chance to pay the fine before the van came to take us to Regina at two o'clock. It was eleven-thirty now. I told him to phone my mother. She was my last — in fact my only — hope to keep me out of jail for 30 days, but as I watched him leave for the phone I was already having second thoughts. When I was in The Hill before I'd told myself that I wanted to have nothing more to with her. That was at least partly because I didn't want to hurt her any more. But I didn't really want to go to jail if I didn't have to. The cop came back to tell me my mother was coming over to see me. I lay back and waited.

When she came we had a very strained conversation. She told me my father would have disowned me long ago. I wanted to scream. She didn't have to bring that type of memory back. It was irrelevant now. But I really didn't want to go to jail if I didn't have to. My mother was going to pay. She just had to make her speech first. We talked very little walking across the street to her house. She went in the back door and said, "I don't want you in my house until you make something of yourself." So that was it. I gathered a few clothes in a duffel bag and walked out to the highway to hitchhike to Regina and then back to Saskatoon. I didn't return for three years. I didn't say good-bye, either.

I was in Regina by three o'clock that afternoon, and sitting in a bar with Calvin. He was telling me how Rob had promised certain death once he got hold of me.

"He's a goof!" I said angrily. That was about the worst insult you could give someone on the street. "He doesn't have the balls to kill me. He just wants to scare me. I'll cut that motherfucker up!" I wanted a fight.

Calvin nodded silently. He could see my wild-eyed expression. I promised to meet him back here at nine o'clock. We were going to an Indian friendship dance.

By chance or by destiny I ran into Rob in the next bar I walked into. He was sitting with some friends. His face was scarred from the stitches to his cheekbones and lips. His nose had healed well.

There wasn't much of a fight. Rob walked up to me as if he wanted to shake my hand and let bygones be bygones. I let him play up to me, but I was alert. His left hand moved suddenly to grab the five-inch hunting knife he'd tucked in the back of his pants. He made a stabbing thrust toward my intestines. I instinctively jumped to the right. At the same time I grabbed his left forearm with both hands and brought it down like a piece of lumber over my knee. It snapped in two. He let out a scream. I threw one punch that caught him in the lips. He flew backwards, holding his mouth with one hand while the other hung bent and limp at his side. I didn't wait for his companions to react. I slipped out the door and down the street and around the corner. Then I leaned against a building and let out a ball of wind that had seemed suspended in my lungs since I first saw the knife. I realized how close I had come once again to getting stabbed.

I made it back to meet Calvin at nine. He was already there. He motioned for me to come and sit down.

"There were two guys in here looking for you, Jim. I think it's about Rob again." His face had a worried expression.

"I told you he was a goof. He can't finish what he started," I replied nonchalantly, and lit up a cigar. I had been smoking for two months. "What about the dance?"

Calvin looked at me for a moment, then remarked cheerfully, "You're another mad dog Indian who's going to kill half his own race over shit like this in the street." He shook his head from side to side. "We'll go to the dance, but try not to break anyone else's arms while we're there, okay?"

We went to the dance and Calvin soon had his choice of women. He was well known and it was cool to be with him. He took a tall Indian princess. She was quiet, but every so often she'd whisper into Calvin's ear, and he'd smile and give her a playful pinch.

I sat and got drunk, then drunker. I started a conversation with the man who ran the bar. He kept giving me shots of straight whisky and rum while he went on about life as a university student. I woke up on the table with the Indian princess shaking me. I could see Calvin shaking his head over her shoulder.

"What time is it?" I mumbled.

"It's two-thirty." Calvin sounded disappointed.

We went in Calvin's car to the princess's place in south Regina. They went to bed while I helped myself at her well-stocked bar. She had bottles of red and white wine, bottles of scotch and rum. Finally I found what I was looking for, a bottle of Canadian Club. I watched some 1940s movie and guzzled the whisky from the bottle. I was going to head back to Saskatoon, make some money, then head for the balmy west coast of America. Make it for the winter, I thought, since August was almost over, and I wanted to get there before my 20th birthday, which was in a month.

I partied in Regina for a few more days, but I was anxious to get back to Saskatoon. I wanted to find out more about my family. I had to know who they were, and who I was. So I borrowed $20 and headed for the highway. That night I was sitting in downtown Saskatoon with Brian and his old lady. I confided in Brian. It was the first time I'd confided in anybody. He listened carefully, nodding occasionally as I told him what I knew and what I thought I knew. Then he smiled gently and started telling me about a guy he'd met in jail who was from Ile-à-la-Crosse. He'd been adopted at a young age, like myself, and had the same last name. He was two years older. He didn't look like me at all, though.

Brian went on to say that he hung around downtown a lot. In fact, he was in the bar the previous night, but of course Brian thought nothing of it. This was the first time he'd heard anything about my past.

I was stunned. I kept asking for details he obviously couldn't provide. But I was obsessed with knowing. I asked him about this guy's brothers and sisters, his parents, his childhood, his upbringing. Brian just shook his head regretfully. He couldn't answer me. He promised to look into it more when he ran into the guy again. I did get one valuable piece of information, though: his name was Randy. As far as Brian knew from talking to him in jail, he had brothers who had been adopted, too, and he was himself pursuing his lost family and childhood.

It shook my own senses realizing how close I was to finding out something at least, and how close I'd been all the time. If I had only said something to Brian earlier I'd probably have been sharing beers with my brother now.

I had made a good score and was walking around with $500 in my pocket. I was consumed with the idea of going to Vancouver and hitching down the coast to Los Angeles. At the same time I was consumed with the idea of finding out who this Randy was. I should have gone to Vancouver.

It was a hot September day when I was getting juiced in the Barry Hotel on Avenue B and Twentieth Street. I'd been thrown out of the bar twice for fighting — in fact I'd been barred for life — but the bouncer wasn't around during the day. I took the opportunity to pour back the beer and rap with the street people making their regular rounds through the bars. They'd sell you anything you could think of. A guy with a little extra money never had to go shopping if he knew enough boosters.

Brian had come in about three, and we'd made plans to do a score that I'd lined up earlier in the week. Brian was unwilling at first, but when he saw me walking around with wads of cash, lots of beer and drugs, the temptation to live it up got to him.

I agreed to meet him back at the bar at nine o'clock. I was supposed to meet a girl at two o'clock, but I was running on Indian time, which meant whenever I got there.

I walked to her place to discover that she didn't like my Indian time, and had left with some other guy at three. It must have been her back-up plan. I ended up staying there with her younger brother and his friends. They had a couple of cases of cold beer and a bag of California Gold weed just waiting to get smoked.

At eight-thirty I realized I had to be back at the bar by nine. It was an hour's walk. Why I didn't take a cab still puzzles me. I had the money. The idea just never surfaced. I'd walked for half a dozen blocks when I came across an appliance store with ghetto blasters displayed in the window. The crime was spontaneous. First I looked for a rock, then I simply kicked out the front door window. I walked in and grabbed two ghetto blasters. I was free. I was across the street. There were no witnesses, no alarms, nothing. I should have walked on and sold the two ghetto blasters and got on with my life. But no, I had to be bolder, more daring. I wanted more money. I went back inside. I was heading back out the window when I saw the policeman standing there, holding his gun. "Hold it right there!" I was history.

I was handcuffed and roughed up, verbally abused, and thrown in the back of the police cruiser. I estimated my sentence would be nine months to a year. I was thrown into the city cells overnight to await court in the morning. I decided just to cop out, get my sentence, and get the hell out of there. I was still thinking of the white sands of California.

I walked to court with 12 other ragged and hung-over inmates who were facing a variety of charges, from break and enter to assault to touching their young daughter's privates. I walked into court when the bailiff called my name. Before the judge had a chance to read out my options I blurted out my plea: guilty. The prosecutor was caught off guard. The judge granted him a short adjournment till two o'clock, at which time

I was to come back and receive my prison term.

I sat back in the cells, wondering what Brian was doing. I thought of Donna and how she had asked me over to her place just two nights ago, after the friendship dance. But she was still 15! She was on my mind a lot. I thought of writing to her once I started doing time. I knew she was going to turn 16 soon. I figured I'd be out by next spring when she was legal. But once again, the system had different plans for me.

The prosecutor scowled as I walked back into court. "Your Honor, we have Mr Tyman's record. As you can see, he has numerous convictions for property-related offenses. Mr Tyman has shown no consideration for other people's property. He has also shown a lack of respect for the law, as you can see by the numerous instances of breach of probation. We ask Your Honor for a lengthy prison term. Thank you."

I wanted to say thank you to the prosecutor for making me look like a desperado from an old western, but I declined. The judge studied my record. He turned his white-haired head toward me and said simply, "Fifteen months in the Saskatoon correctional center. Dismissed." When I walked into the correctional center, I was not expecting what I found. I'd been informed of it by local street people and by a few ex-cons, but I was still speechless. You just don't expect to see 120 pound females walking around looking like guards, acting like guards, and really being guards.

This was not the kind of jail I was used to. People were wearing their own clothes. There were no noisy inmates yelling from tier to tier, no gangs of inmates spreading terror and mayhem. The thing that really struck me numb was the fact that the Saskatoon Correctional Center had no protective custody range. The skinners and diddlers (child molesters), the stool pigeons, and the plain goofs were all in main population. The place was a haven for the undesirables of the correctional system. If the Regina Correctional Center was a Pit Bull, the Saskatoon Correctional Center was a French Poodle with no teeth. I had trouble adjusting to the mellow atmosphere.

I was taken to Unit B-1, which had a pool room and a ping-pong table. The cells were more like bedrooms. You had your own desk, your own closet. You had a window. You even had your own key to open and lock your door whenever you felt like it. It made me smile. This was heaven for doing time.

I was not in my glory long, though. When I played my first game of floor hockey, of course I ran over the first guy who got in my way. The rest of the inmates started threatening me. The guard told me someone might get hurt playing rough like that. I couldn't believe it. I laughed at them and went to the weight room.

I started having other problems with the "new vision" the government was introducing into the correctional system. I was used to the hard and the bitter. This was flowers and candy. The units were equipped with such luxuries as a fridge and stove. Inmates were allowed to cook at specified times. Just when I was getting used to that, I saw one inmate proudly delivering a plate of eggs and bacon to the guards' office. It was earth-shaking. You didn't talk to the screws, let alone make them bacon and eggs! At least, that's what I'd learned in Regina.

I didn't want to talk to any inmate I didn't know. They were making the guards dinner and snacks. The guards were having dinner with the inmates. They'd sit and discuss life like good friends. They sure as hell weren't my friends. I'd listen to the inmates discuss "the skinner who lived in Unit A" or "the stool pigeon who put my buddy in jail. Now I have to work with him." I shook my head. "Go rip the motherfucker's head off if he bugs you that much," I wanted to tell them, but I figured they'd tell their friends the screws that I was acting aggressively.

I wasn't in the unit long before I was formally charged with disobeying a direct order. At count times inmates were required to be on the main floor and nowhere else. I was standing on a landing three steps up a flight of stairs when a snooty young female guard demanded that I come down those last three steps for the count.

"Hey," I said, "I'm right here, so quit this bullshit."

"Look, Mr Tyman, you are required by policy to be on the main floor!" She was pointing at me like a mother scolding a kid. "You come down those steps right now! That is a direct order!"

I laughed and walked back upstairs to watch TV. Ten minutes later I was handed the charge sheet. I was given an aggressive warning by the ADD at kangaroo court. I smiled at him, thought how ludicrous the charge was, and walked out the door. I was back in a week.

I was playing pool when I missed a straight-in shot that cost me the game. When you're around street people and in jail, swearing is as common as the sunrise. I swore loud and long. It so happened there was a guard outside the door. He came storming into the game room. "You're on charge for using profane and offensive language."

Once again I was stumped. "This is fuckin' jail pal. Where do you thinking you're working, fuckin' daycare?"

"Don't fucking push it, Tyman."

I was fooling around in the gymnasium with a floor hockey stick and puck when I got the urge to slap the puck at the female guard. Bad idea. It caught her just above the knee. She almost collapsed when it hit her, but she was a big woman. I was sure I was looking at another couple of months' jail time for assaulting a guard, but with quick thinking I told her I had just wanted to scare her. Either she bought it or she was too scared to cause me any more grief. She spoke to the kangaroo court before I went in. I was kicked out of the gym for five days. She limped around the unit for three weeks. We got along fine after that.

The number of female guards at the Saskatoon Correctional Center caused numerous rumors about their inner needs being satisfied by the inmates, or by their fellow male guards. I was naive at first, but I was taken with the idea of a female staffer coming into my room late at night and fulfilling her desires. It never happened to me, but I'd been in the unit two months when I noticed one guard kept going into this Indian's room. He filled me in on the details later. She came on to him. He said he was nervous at first, for fear of being set up on a sexual assault charge. But after she grabbed his testicles and whispered to him not to worry, he went for it. What happened after that is typical of guard-inmate confrontations. Another guard caught on to it. She made the same kind of advances, but this time she charged him with assault. The guard who started it was promoted.

I made friends with a young white guy in another unit. He'd get seductive smiles from this one female guard whenever we walked around the jogging track. He confided one day that he was in love with her. She was wiser than her colleague, though. She'd waited till the youth got out of jail, then she went over to his place and whoopee! It went on until his present incarceration, and now they were back to their old roles. He said she acted like a mother to him, promising him a good life if he stayed with her. It sounded familiar.

* * *

I spent my 20th birthday in jail. Now Christmas was approaching. It was going to be my first Chistmas in jail, but not my last. I was also headed for court to answer the charge of stealing the girl's bike. I'd had it postponed because I wanted to get out of jail for the day, even if it was only to go to court.

My release date was set for July 15 1984 — until I went to court for the bike. I was expecting to get a sentence that ran concurrently with my present sentence of 15 months. The system didn't agree. The judge looked as if someone had just told him that Charles Manson had moved in next door. "Ninety days consecutive to any sentence you are serving now. Dismissed."

I had to be nudged to start moving. I couldn't believe the sentence. The maximum was 120 days. "This is getting a little carried away," I commented to the escorting police officer.

He snorted with laughter. "I've been a cop for 10 years, and I've never seen a sentence much higher than seven days for what you did."

It did nothing for my attitude, either. I hated authority. I had no respect for anyone who was trying to use his position to get me to do something. But when you're in jail there's no choice. It's a way of life. In Saskatoon, particularly, I had a great deal of trouble taking the female staff seriously. After all, I was over six feet tall. I weighed 225 pounds. When a 120 pound female was scolding me, I tended to laugh in her face, which of course made it worse. I had had knives pulled on me, I'd fought in bars, drunk with pimps and pros, used foul language with every sentence, and now some female who probably breaks down over a soap opera is doing her best to belittle me over some minor infraction. When they tried to act tough — a requirement necessary to be a guard — it just didn't work.

It finally came to a head in January 1984. I was headed for kangaroo court, charged with disobeying a direct order, I believe for the seventh time. I was yawning, and the ADD was appalled.

"You think this is a joke!?"

I looked at him for a moment. "In all honesty, sir, yes."

His hands were shaking as he dialed the Secure Unit. (The government's new vision also meant new names; the Secure Unit was simply the hole.) "I want an escort right now!"

"Watch your blood pressure, sir."

He couldn't speak when Secure Unit staff came to get me. He just motioned to them to take me away.

"See you later, sir." I smiled as I walked out of the office, handcuffed and headed for the hole.

I was confined for 10 days. I was also removed from Unit B-1 for racist and aggressive behavior. I was going to be moved to overflow dorms. Then the administration was going to decide what to do with me. Overflow dorms are the same thing as North G in Regina, but a hell of a lot cleaner.

I wasn't in overflow long before I was charged with using

profane language again. I think I was charged half a dozen times for using foul language in jail. Sounds a bit ironic. But this time I was whisked away to Semi-Secure Unit. It was the center's jail within a jail.

Semi-Secure Unit is half the hole. You're locked up 11 hours out of 24: eight during the night and three during the day. If you're lucky enough to get a job with the main population, then you avoid being locked up. But jobs were hard to come by in Semi. When the administration moved you to Semi, they made it clear they wanted nothing to do with you, which was great. I wanted nothing to do with them.

I enjoyed Semi. The guards never left their bubble. You didn't have to eat dinner with them. The inmates weren't their friends. Swearing was commonplace. A blind eye was turned on drug use. Fighting among ourselves was fine as long as it stayed among ourselves. Semi-Secure, to me, was jail. The units bore no resemblance to what I thought jail was, and everyone in Semi-Secure thought the same: "Fuck them units. There's nothing but stool pigeons and goofs running around out there, anyway. Fuck them!"

There were 14 inmates confined to Semi, and we acted like a small family. Inmates confined to Semi never wanted to leave, even though all the privileges were out in main population. There was more freedom out there, there was late night television, there was a chance of early release. But the female guards, the goof inmates, the ludicrous enforcement of rules, were just too much to put up with.

I enjoyed Semi for another reason: we played floor hockey every night, and you could hit other players without some guard or inmate telling you to take it easy.

The government introduced a program at that time which caught my interest. If you were sent to one of the jail work camps, usually located in the parks, you would earn one day off your sentence for every five days you worked. I started inquiring about my chances.

"Your attitude, Jim."

"What the fuck is wrong with my attitude?"

"Right there, see, you swore. That's not good."

"I swore?" I muffled a laugh. "Where the fuck do you think I am? And what the fuck do you think I did to get in here? I never said I was peaches and cream, pal. All I want is to go to camp. If I fuck up, fine. But all I want is to work my ass off and be left alone. So what's the problem with that?"

"I'll have to talk to Piska, Jim."

Piska was head of security. I wasn't sure where I stood with him. I figured it wasn't good, but I was moved to overflow with the promise that I'd be sent to a unit for more analysis. I was told that if my behavior was good, Piska had authorized my camp placement.

I went to Unit A-1 this time. I was there two days. I was warned by the guards several times about my aggressive behavior (I had sworn out loud). I thought, "If you want aggressive behavior, I'll show you aggressive behavior. I'll snap that pretty neck of yours. Then you can say I was aggressive." But I would bite my tongue or go to the gym and hit the punching bag. I wanted to rap a few guards and inmates upside the head my first few days. I was set to tell them to take me back to Semi and stick their camp, but I was informed that afternoon that after 30 charge-free and incident-free days I would be off to camp. I had new hope. I had just under four months left, and with the one day off for five day's work, I could chop that down to just over three. I'd be out in the first week of August of 1984.

The camp for the correctional center was 60 miles straight south, by the Gardiner Dam on Lake Diefenbaker, in Danielson Provincial Park. It was April when one of the camp staff came to pick me up. The camp was run by a big man with the biggest mouth and the biggest case of self-centeredness I have ever seen. The man I'm sure believed he was put on earth to render justice — his way or no way.

You get used to egotistical people in jail. The guards carry themselves like lords, and so do some of the inmates. Beats me why. For people supposedly at the bottom of the social ladder, they sure don't act that way. But I've never seen anything to compare with the arrogance of the Danielson Camp manager. He was the pinnacle of purity, he was the hero, he was a superstar athlete, he was a lady killer, he was everything you weren't. Just ask him. He'd sit you down and tell you how he'd won the game for the team, how he was the toughest guy on the block. He was a walking legend. Something else that made the man wonderful to be around was the fact that we came from the same town, a fact he brought up on our first encounter.

"I'll have you know that I will not have any shit like you were pulling in Saskatoon at my camp, Tyman!"

It was six-thirty in the morning. I had just arrived last night. I wasn't even sure who this guy was yet, but Al Draker let me know right away.

"I'm not racist one iota, Tyman!" He paused to let me smell his morning breath. "I'll have you know my wife is a native, so don't come on to me that I'm a racist! Because Al Draker is not racist!" He slammed the desk with the palm of his hand. "Do I make myself clear?"

Not really, Al Draker, but good morning anyway. "Why are you telling me this?"

"Because I understand you're a racist, and I won't have any racist shit at my camp!"

"Well, Al Draker," I said, "my mama is whiter than you'll ever be, so if I hate honkies, I must hate my mama. Or do I?" I shrugged and smiled. Bad move.

He bolted to his feet, and roared with every air sac his lungs could empty. "Don't get smart in my camp, Tyman!" His sausage finger was inches from my face. "I know who you are. You were just a snot-nosed kid when I was finishing high school!"

I studied him for a minute. He was grinning. "You're from Fort Qu'Appelle, I take it."

He sucked in his gut, ran his hands through his hair, and sat back down, still grinning. "That's right. I used to live a block away from you when you lived across from the school." He snickered. "I knocked out your brother's teeth playing football."

"I almost knocked them out not playing football."

We stared at each other for a few moments. "I can see we're going to have a lot of fun together. Yes sirree." He let out a small whistle.

"Well geez, I hope so, Al."

His face turned a nice, bright red. "Do you want to go back to the center?"

"What for, Al?" I stretched out my hands.

Al didn't know what to say. I kept grinning at him. He got madder. Finally he waved me out of the office. "Go have breakfast."

"Sure, Al. Nice meeting you." I held out my hand. He didn't shake it.

I walked to the mess hall pondering what my new friend had said about me being a racist. I smiled to myself. I'd been a good Indian, a scummy Indian, an apple, and now a racist Indian. What would tomorrow bring? But if Al Draker wanted to send me back to the correctional center with a major report on my racist movements, I was going to be a model inmate. That way he could see my smiling face for the next three months.

There was a fight out at camp one day. I wasn't even aware of it till I came back from my work assignment 15 miles away. Al had called a meeting of all inmates and staff. He was beautiful.

"I understand we have serious tension between whites and natives!" he roared. "I won't have any such shit at my camp! My wife is native, I'm not racist!" I was glad there was no desk for him to pound. "Any of you guys want to go back to the center, pack your things! You're going back this afternoon! Tyman, Arcand, Wolfe, and Bugler, come to my office!"

We went to his office.

"What the hell is going on, Tyman?"

I was stumped. I didn't even know who was fighting. "What do you mean?"

"You know what I damn well mean! What's this racist shit going on out here? Do you want to go back?"

He almost had me. I almost let him win. But I bit my lip and shook my head.

"What about the rest of you?" He glared at the other three Indians in the office. They had seen the way Al handled the camp. They'd had enough of him. They all agreed to go back.

What was strange about this was that Al was willing to send back four Indians because of supposed tension between the races, but no whites. What really happened that day was this: a known stool pigeon had been punched once in the mouth. He ran back to camp from his work placement a mile away and told the staff that the Indians were rampaging. Maybe some of us felt like it, but all he did — and I believe he knew what he was doing — was add more fuel to Draker's racist theory.

Draker was set at any time to ship me back to jail with a report on the Indian uprising. It was his obsession. But one thing I can say for Al Draker is that he was an honest person. He could easily have sent me back on some pretext or other. But he never did. I was expecting it, in fact, but the man was honorable in that sense.

I was digging a trench for a water line when he drove up in his truck. He wore his best stone face for me. "You're getting out Monday."

I had calculated that my release date was still two weeks away. I was confused. "What do you mean?"

"The government has extended the early release to 21 days, so anyone who was getting the regular 15 days now gets the 21. Congratulations, Tyman." He roared away, leaving me in his dust.

I sat in Overflow Three. Actually, I paced in Overflow Three. I was getting out the next morning. Al had sent me back the afternoon he told me. He had no reason to, but I didn't care. I had another sleepless night, but the life surged through me in the morning. It had been 11 months since I was on the streets.

It was a Saturday morning when the center staff drove me

and two other inmates to the bus depot. I phoned the adulteress. She came and picked me up, plus my garbage bag full of everything I owned. I had a few drinks with her, but she could see my restlessness. I wanted to hit Twentieth Street, find a woman and, more important, pick up a hundred lot of acid. I was going to sell dope for a living.

That night I was dancing up a storm in a downtown hotel, pouring back the beer, yelling across at other ex-cons I saw, and making raw advances toward the female I had found sitting alone in the bar. The next night I found myself in a rather uneasy predicament. I wanted to look up Donna. She was 16 now. I couldn't explain it to myself. I'd never had much trouble finding a girl, but for some reason I wanted 16 year old Donna Nighttraveller.

The girl I had picked up the night before still clung to my side. I was set to tell her to hit the road and thanks for the good times and we'll see you again. But I had told her my plans that morning, and she sensed what I was trying to do when I told her to go home. She didn't want to leave me.

"I know where to get some acid," she said. "No problem. Cheap also." She stood smiling away.

"Okay then, let's check it out."

She took me to a house on the east side of Saskatoon. It was middle class, owned by white people who looked incredulously at each other when I walked through the front door. I purchased 100 hits of yellow micro-dot acid for $300. It was a bit more than the going rate, but I was in a hurry, and arguing with white people over $50 was no part of my early release plans. If I sold it all, I could make a couple of hundred easy bucks. Acid was a hot commodity on the street.

I took her to a movie Sunday night, then I took her to the adulteress's. She had helped me get my acid; it would have been rude to send her on her way. Monday afternoon I finally convinced her to go home, promising that I'd phone her at nine o'clock. I had no intention of keeping that promise.

I met a former con in the Albany Hotel down on Twentieth

and B, just across from the Barry. He was considered a waterhead in jail, a general fuck-up, but I was going to use him for selling my acid. In return I'd buy him a few beers over the course of the evening.

I'd made a couple of hundred dollars already, and I was drunk to boot. My companion was busy running around the bar selling the tablets of acid. I had a solid reputation in jail, and he knew it was good to be associated with me, so he gladly ran errands for me while I sat and talked with girls and fellow ex-cons, and planned how to make more cash.

Things were going well. I was already planning another buy of acid when another ex-con came to me and told me of an easy score he had planned. With the prospect of easy cash, and the excitement of the alcohol in me, we ventured to a fur store in his van. We were going to make thousands.

The score was easy. I was going to go in through a side window and pop open the back door. We were each going to grab a handful of coats, and be on our way. I was in the store and had an armful already. My heart was racing. The thought of how crazy it was to be doing this suddenly dawned on me. I raced to the back door. I fumbled and cursed, but I undid the dead bolts and latches. I flung open the door, and there stood two cops. I had been out of jail for 60 hours.

* * *

Talk about depression. Sure, I had no one to blame but myself. But imagine sitting in jail with charges of break and enter, possession of a restricted drug for the purpose of trafficking, and simple possession of cannabis resin, for I had some hash oil on me at the time also. And I had just got out 60 hours ago, after serving 11 months.

I lay on the mattress, again trying to estimate my sentence. Two years was my prediction for the break and enter. But the drug charges played havoc with my insides. The cops had me with 43 hits of acid, a roll of $5.00 bills (the going rate for acid) that could choke a horse, plus my previous record of drug use. It didn't look good. I tossed and turned. My best hope was that when it was all over I'd end up with a three-year sentence for everything.

This time the prosecutor was ready for me. I pleaded guilty to the break and enter. The judge looked almost sorry for me when he was informed that I had just got out of jail for a similar charge. The prosecutor had to clear his throat twice before asking for two years. Even he felt a bit sorry for me.

"Eighteen months in Saskatoon Correctional Center. Appear in two weeks to enter a plea on the drug charges. Dismissed."

I walked back to the holding area of the courthouse. I was lucky with the 18 months, but the drug charges were easily going to shoot my sentence up to three years.

I got ribbed by my fellow cons for coming back so soon. They asked me how I enjoyed my TA — Temporary Absence — and when I was going to the pen. The administration was just as surprised to see me back, but after three days in overflow they put me back in Semi-Secure. (I was classified as medium security, due to the outstanding charges.) In their minds I was already convicted and sentenced on the drug charges.

I had many sleepless nights awaiting my preliminary hearing. I'd walk up and down the range, back and forth. The other cons would sit me down and give me some tokes of marijuana so I could relax enough to talk about it. I was planning to beat the rap now. Sure, the cops had found all the drugs, but they'd found them in my vest. I wasn't wearing it at the time. It was on the fence behind the fur store. I was not actually in possession of the drugs, and I was positive the police couldn't prove it was my vest. That was my only hope.

Then one day they sent it back to me. I had just got back from work in the mechanics shop when the bull called me to the bubble. He had a parcel for me: my leather vest.

"Look, man! I got them motherfuckers now!" I told my bewildered neighbor about the blunder the police had made.

"Yeah, I see, Jimmy. But why're you so excited about a vest? It looks old, anyway."

"Don't you see, bro? This is the vest they found the drugs in. Now when I go to my prelim in December, what are they going to say? 'We found the acid in Mr Tyman's vest, and the money also.' Then my lawyer simply asks them, 'Where is the vest?'"

"You son of a bitch!" He was smiling now. "You beat them again." He grabbed my hand. "Way to go, Jimmy!"

Relief. Now I waited for the formalities. I waited for my lawyer to tell me the charges were being either dropped or stayed, which means they have a year to retry. I was removed from Semi and placed in Unit C-1. I figured the police had informed the center that I wasn't going anywhere; I'd be at the center for the remainder of my sentence.

My lawyer phoned me two weeks before my prelim: "Jim, we have a deal."

"Yeah?" I felt the excitement flowing through me.

"Plead guilty to simple possession of a restricted drug and possession of the hash oil, and the crown will give you three to five months consecutive."

I made my decision. "I'll take the time."

So now the waiting game started. I'd been scheduled for release in August 1985; that would probably be moved up to October, if not later. I had at least another 10 months to go. I was going to have three birthdays in jail. I was 19 when I came in and I'd be 22 when I got out; my old school chums would probably be just starting their careers, maybe getting married, or having their first child.

I wrote to my mother while I was inside. She was supportive and understanding. She wished me well and hoped for my future. She never failed to send me birthday and Christmas cards. I thought of how I had screwed up a good relationship with her. I thought of my biological family. Sure, they were my "real" family, but the Tymans had looked after me for as long as I could remember. I knew the pain I must have caused them — and the guilt it was causing me. I tried to replay my life. Where did I go wrong? Why am I here? Where will I be in a year? Two years? Jail? Dead? The nuthouse?

At night I would look out my cell window at the flickering lights of Saskatoon. I could see houses being built in a new residential area. Life was continuing. The people out there had careers, a future, something. I had nothing but my balls. I could rob and corrupt, but deep within me I didn't want to. I wanted what I could see from my window: a home, a family, some real love, just something. But what I saw in my future was the exact opposite: crime, violence, drugs, booze, and an early death. I didn't know how to change. I wanted to, but whenever I made plans for a better future, I'd get frustrated and go back to my motto: "Fuck it!"

I wrote to Donna often. I felt something when I wrote to her. It was strange. I'd never been to bed with her. I'd never done anything with her. I hadn't even seen her for over a year! But when I thought of her, there was a closeness. I started to confide in her. I told her about the past. I told her how I'd screwed up a good thing with my family. I told her about the deep hatred inside me. I wrote a poem, short but to the point:

Life is great
When you're full of hate.

I went to court in December. It was rehearsed, I'm positive. The judge came in. He listened to the prosecutor. He listened to my legal aid lawyer. He nodded and shuffled his papers. He put his hand to his chin. He said, "Three months consecutive to any sentence you are now serving, and 30 days concurrent for the cannabis resin charge. Dismissed."

My release date was October 25, 1985, by which time I would have served two years and seven weeks (minus 60 hours) in a place where the average stay was four months.

* * *

Time dragged on, the usual prison grind, 16 months of the same old bullshit. I was getting restless. I started arguing with the mechanics shop boss about the few rules he enforced, and finally he kicked me out of his shop. By that time I'd also been sent back to Semi-Secure, with a directive from the head of security that I was never to be let into population again. I had told one female staffer that if she was any prettier she could work for me once I got out of jail. She was not impressed.

The head of the education program had me confined during work hours, which meant 16 hours a day. He was not about to give me another job. No one wanted me. So I made other plans. I was fed up with the system, the screws, the inmates. In February I spoke to my corrections officer.

"It's like this, pal. You guys won't give me a job, and now you lock me up all day for not working! You won't move me to a unit, even though I'm low security! Why? Because you've got a pile of bleeding heart females and skin hounds and goofs who tell your staff members that I'm threatening their well-being. Well, fuck this! Send me to Secure, then you can all forget about me, and I can forget about you!"

"C'mon, Jim." He was surprisingly cool. "Just let management cool their heads a while, and we'll find you work."

But I'd had 16 and a half months of this bullshit. I'd had enough of the head games, the power-tripping screws, the waterhead inmates. There were ice cubes all over (waterheads acting solid) and I'd had enough of them. "You move me," I said, "or I'll burn the fuckin' unit down!" I was in Secure within half an hour.

I was locked up 21 hours a day. My security rating was low, but I wanted nothing to do with the system, and they wanted nothing to do with me. I concluded that this was best for both parties. I wouldn't talk to staff when they brought my food. They sent down staff I was known to get along with, but I wouldn't talk to them, either. They were all part of the system. They were the enemy.

I spent two months in the hole. For the first month I was asked every week if I was ready to go back to Semi. Each time I declined. Finally I was told just to ask when I wanted to go back. I would probably have stayed in the hole till my time was up, but my love of hockey got to me. I was let out to watch TV from seven-thirty till nine o'clock, and it was maddening to have to leave a playoff game in the middle of the third period. I asked to be put back in Semi. The next day I was.

I wasn't back an hour before I noticed something that both excited and puzzled me: my release date was wrong. When you're in Semi, as well as Secure, the guards have your name up on a chalkboard in their bubble. When I got to Semi I looked at my name and my release date, for no particular reason. It said June 21st, 1985 — four months before I was due to be released.

I thought it must be a mistake, or a bad joke, so I let on that I didn't notice. But the weeks went by and the date never changed. One day I had to make sure.

"Hey Turcotte, my release date is wrong."

"Yeah?"

"Yeah. It should be June 15th, not the 21st. I earned a few days at camp. You guys fucked up as usual." I smiled at him. He sighed and went to look at the computer printout. If it was on the printout, it was right.

"Sorry, Jim. Your release date is the 21st."

I couldn't believe my ears. I demanded to see the printout. Again he sighed, but he ripped it off the machine. He pointed to my name. It said the 21st. I could feel the adrenalin running through me. June 21st was in four weeks!

I paced my cell. I was sure they were going to find out. How could they screw up so badly? I wasn't going to tell anyone about it. The stool pigeons would be tripping over themselves to tell the screws. I remained silent till June 20th at nine o'clock at night.

"You know," I said to a friend down in Semi, "I'm not supposed to get out tomorrow."

He looked wide-eyed at me. "You shitting me, man?"

"No, my friend. They fucked up, and now I get out with no restrictions." We roared with laughter at the thought of the government losing four months of my sentence somewhere.

I was packed and ready to go the next morning. I was still inclined to believe that they knew, and that they'd all have a good laugh when I got to admitting and discharge. I sipped my morning coffee with my friend.

"Are you ready, Tyman?" The screw stood smiling away.

"As soon as I finish my coffee." I smiled back at him. He was amazed that I didn't jump to my feet.

"They're waiting for you, Jim."

"Let them wait. I want to finish my coffee."

My friend spoke up: "C'mon, Jim. Get your brown ass outta here!" We shook hands. I winked at him. I walked to admitting.

I was alone with the head of admitting and discharge. I was expecting the cocky smile, and, "Do you think we're stupid?" Or: "You thought you had us, eh Tyman?" Instead, he said, "Sign here." I signed there.

"Okay Jim, let's go." It was my escorting guard from Semi; he was taking me to the front of the prison. I was incredulous. The electronic steel doors opened one at a time, and I was out. I felt light-headed. I was free!

I waited centuries for the adulteress to drive up. I tried cracking jokes with the guard. Either he wasn't in the mood or my jokes were bad. I kept shooting glances at the steel doors. I was waiting for the goon squad to come racing through, handcuffs ready, smiles pasted on, and I'd be whisked back inside. But it didn't happen. The guard got tired of waiting. He mumbled good luck and walked back inside.

The adulteress drove up. I jumped in the car. It felt like a getaway from the scene of a crime. I told her to hurry up. Let's move! She told me to relax, it's over. I looked back as we drove out of the prison parking lot. "This is my last laugh, motherfuckers!" We turned the corner. The street awaited me.

JUNE 24th, 1985

I went through a handful of phone numbers and addresses I'd

been given by people in the bars. Some were ex-cons, others were women, others left me in a fog. Finally I found the number I'd been waiting to dial for months: Donna Nighttraveller's.

"Hey Donna! How're you doing?"

"When did you get out?"

"Three days ago. What're you up to?"

"Sitting around, waiting for a call from someone."

"Well, I'm someone. You want to go out for a few drinks with me? You know, celebrate my freedom."

"You know where I live. Come on over."

Donna was 17 now, and I was 21. She lived with her mom in Confederation Park, right on the edge of the city. I stood in her doorway, hot and tired. "How're you doing, Donna?"

She smiled broadly. She was looking fine. "Well, well. Come in and sit down. I'll get ready."

I wasn't sure if Donna was into the downtown scene any more. When she spoke of downtown she seemed contemptuous of the people and their ways. I didn't want to upset her. We went to bars I knew she would like. At a nightclub on Idylwyld Drive I sat sipping whisky and just watching her dance. Boy, that girl could dance!

We walked the streets after the bar closed. We talked about what she had done since I was in, what I did while I was in, what I was planning to do now. We walked to Twenty-Second Street. I had some marijuana, so we stopped and smoked a joint. "What are you smiling about?" she asked.

"Oh well ..." I didn't finish. I took her head between my hands, pulled her toward me, and kissed her on the lips. She was startled at first. Our eyes locked. Then we kissed again. We walked for 10 minutes, stopped and necked some more. There was an apartment building off Twenty-Second where we smoked another few joints. We necked in the shadows. The moment didn't seem wrong. We made love in the darkness.

* * *

I was staying in the basement of the adulteress's house. She had two kids: a robust boy and a sassy little girl of nine. She had two sisters staying with her also, plus a couple of boarders, so the house was full all the time. We all had one thing in common: we liked to party. When I brought Donna over to this house full of drinkers, she was immediately accepted as one of the crowd. She ended up staying with me. It just happened. We had been seeing each other for a month now, and suddenly it dawned on me that Donna had spent only a few nights at home since I got out. She wouldn't admit it, but we were shacked up.

I spent the first month out relatively calm. I'd go downtown to see a group of pimps and pros I was making friends with, while Donna went out to nightclubs to dance her heart away. Sometimes I brought her downtown to meet my type of people, but most of the time she didn't want to come. She didn't like the downtown scene any more. She wouldn't give me specifics, but I believe the violence just flatly turned her off and frightened her.

By the second month I'd made good friends with a local pimp named Harry. He was as big and as crazy as I was. We'd drink and yell around the bars together. He liked to pour back the bottle just as hard as I did. We'd roam the bar while he looked for someone for me to fight. He'd spot him, point him out, and I would proceed to fight. I was crazy, no doubt about it. I packed a machete inside my jacket, plus a folding hunting knife in my back pocket. I never used them, but I was ready should someone pull a knife on me. I slept with knives tucked under my pillow, or within grabbing distance of my bed. I was picking fights with lots of people. I never had to use a knife. But the thought of them coming to avenge themselves was always on my mind. I knew what I would do if I were them.

I was sitting in the bar of the Albany Hotel when I spotted a guy who for one reason or another was threatening to do me in. The guy was a waterhead and a plain big mouth. One night he'd run into Donna in another bar and had started threatening her because of me. Bad mistake. I walked up and asked him what his problem was. He pushed me against the wall. So began the chase. I had one thing in mind: I was going to ram my blade right through to his spine. It started at the Albany. I followed him to the Windsor Hotel. From there he took off to the Capri Hotel, where I finally got my sights on him. I had my knife out already, and it was arcing up toward his abdomen.

"He's got a knife!" he shrieked. The bartender, who was right behind me, heard him and grabbed my arm. It didn't stop the thrust, but it slowed it down enough to save him. The blade fell short by inches.

The patrons escorted me out of the bar. I reached the street in time to see the police cruisers come screeching around the corner. There was a prostitute coming down the street. I threw her my knife. She picked it up and tucked it in her purse just as a burly cop flung me face-first against the wall.

The guy who almost digested my knife came screaming out of the bar, demanding that I be frisked. "He's got a knife, officer! He's got a knife!" They checked me out, frisked me down. I glanced at the prostitute. She gave me a wink and a smile. I smiled back. I told the cops the guy was plain crazy. They shrugged. What could they do? They were about to leave the scene when the guy decided to start a fist fight with me. It was funny, actually. I ducked and side-stepped two of his punches. The third was stopped by the cops, who tackled and handcuffed him. He was whisked off to jail. The prostitute smiled and gave me back the knife.

I realized later what had happened: I had been ready to stab this man in front of 50 witnesses. All he wanted was a fist fight, but I wanted to hurt him badly. I was getting more violent. I used to have doubts about whether I could shank another human being, but now it was obvious: I didn't care.

People heard about my escapade, so naturally I got a reputation. In street life a reputation for using a knife earns you respect. Now I was getting respect, and I was meeting more people heavily involved in street life. There was a war between pimps at that time, and I found myself between two sides. All

I wanted was to party and let the good times roll. But as time passed it became obvious that I'd better stick to one group, for the pimp war was escalating. Tensions were building. Knifings were common. People like me, who weren't really involved, were getting murdered. Finally one night gun shots erupted in the Baldwin Hotel. Luckily, no one was killed. But after the smoke cleared, nine people were arrested. I was arrested the same night for a robbery I knew nothing about. It was late October, and I was back in jail while Donna raised the money for my bail.

I was held in the remand section of the Saskatoon Correctional Center. There are two remand units in the jail. I was placed in Remand One. All my buddies were in Remand Two. As far as the pimps in Remand One were concerned, I was a spy for the other side. When they arrested everyone they naturally split them up, but to this day I'm positive that putting me in a dangerous situation like that was the administration's idea of teaching me a lesson. I had already been attacked once on the street by one of these guys in Remand One; he came at me with a hammer. I'd also lost the use of one finger over this pimp war — nine stitches, and it didn't heal for six months. There were knives down there, and I was alert every minute. But I didn't expect them to make a move on me in jail. It would be stupid. Even so, the 30 days I was there awaiting the money for my bail were the most uneasy I've spent behind bars.

On payment of $500 I was finally released on bail supervision, with the conditions that I report three times a week to a bail officer, abide by a curfew from ten at night till seven in the morning, refrain from alcohol, stay out of liquor stores or business premises where the main purpose is to sell alcohol, keep the peace and be of good behavior, and attend court when told to do so. If I had been convicted and released on parole, I would have had less restrictions.

Donna and I had moved out of the adulteress's basement into an apartment in Fairhaven, which we were sharing with various other people. I wasn't happy. I had a pile of restrictions, my buddies were all in jail, and I was broke. Donna suggested I start looking for my real family again. I was interested, but I didn't know where to start.

"Try Social Services," Donna suggested.

I called them. "I'm sorry, that is privileged government information," an elderly sounding woman told me over the phone.

"Privileged?" I shot back at her. "Privileged! We're talking about my family, not yours, lady."

"I'm sorry, Mr Tyman, we can't help you." She kept her composure. "It's government policy." I slammed the phone down.

"What's the matter, Jim?" Donna looked worried.

"The government is the problem! They do nothing but make rules to frustrate you. Why can't they show you the way once in a while, instead of always trying to divert you?"

I leaned back and closed my eyes. Donna came over to comfort me. I was in love with her, I realized. I'd never told her. It seemed odd for me to say something like that.

"Hey, Donna," I whispered as I stroked her hair.

"Yeah?" she replied softly as she nestled her head against my chest.

"I love you. I mean ... yeah, Donna. I really love you."

She looked up at me and smiled. "I love you also, James Tyman."

* * *

Donna had friends who were in adult upgrading classes. They had a Christmas party scheduled for December 20th, and I was asked to attend with her. All my buddies were in jail, so I thought I'd have a good time with people who were trying to make a life for themselves. I also figured these guys should be mellow. I could leave my knives at home and enjoy myself.

The party was in southwest Saskatoon, in a clubhouse the school had rented for the evening. I recognized a lot of people when I walked in. There was a guy named Carmen and a few others I knew from downtown. There were a lot of Donna's friends who I'd met over the past several months, and a pack of high school dropouts, the type of people I was used to being around in Fort Qu'Appelle. They were now attending adult upgrading classes, and they were fascinated by my stories of jail and my nomadic lifestyle.

Carmen was busily trying to seduce a young woman. Her ex-boyfriend was also there — Terry Sabadash, or the Sab, as he liked to be called. He was as tall as me but about 40 pounds lighter. He wasn't as impressed with Carmen's stories as his former girlfriend was. He started in first on his ex. He was going to start in on Carmen when I intervened. I told him to have a few beer and leave the lovebirds alone. He walked away to sulk in a corner. About half an hour later the Sab's buddy Glen decided he could beat me up. He was five foot seven and weighed about 140 soaking wet. He was drunk and full of bravado. To my embarrassment, I found myself going outside with him.

A group of people came with us, trying to dissuade Glen from making a fool of himself, but he was like a dog with a bone. I dropped him with a quick left and a right, then walked away. He started a pushing match with someone smaller right away. I was walking back inside, buttoning my shirt — Glen had ripped it open as he fell to the ground — when out came the Sab. He walked by and elbowed me in the ribs. I wasn't going to ruin an otherwise good party by starting with him, so I sighed to myself and let him go. Only when I walked into the light of the clubhouse did I see the hole below my ribs. The blood started pumping immediately.

"That fucker stabbed me!" I instinctively reached for my knife. It wasn't there. I'd left it at home. "Carmen, give me your shank! I'm going to carve that bastard up!"

Carmen wasn't sure what had happened. Then he saw the hole below my ribs. He grabbed a pool cue. A couple of other friends grabbed steel bars. Carmen shouted to me as he went outside: "Stay inside, Jim! We'll get that son of a bitch!"

I was still shouting at someone to give me a shank, but school kids don't usually pack knives to a Christmas party. I was left staring at a crowd of frightened faces. I watched as Carmen and his friends confronted Sabadash. He was trying to say it wasn't their beef. But Carmen was a friend from downtown, and you have a special bond with a guy like that. The Sab ducked as the pool cue swooshed over his head. Then he saw four people come at him, and he took off at a gallop. Good plan. They chased him for 10 blocks, but he finally eluded them in an industrial yard full of culverts and pipes and other sewage equipment.

I studied the hole below my ribs. Donna came over, obviously worried. "You should go to the hospital, Jim." She spoke quietly as she wiped away the blood that dripped down my abdomen.

I was still steamed about getting knifed. "It doesn't hurt," I said. It didn't, either. It felt numb.

I walked to the bar and drank a few shots of whisky to calm myself. People came up to ask if they should phone the cops or an ambulance. I told them to forget it, it didn't hurt. Then it started to hurt. I suddenly got a cramp-like feeling in my gut. I buckled over.

"I think I'd better go to the hospital," I said, and within seconds I was in the back seat of a Camaro, racing down Circle Drive at speeds close to 100. We were heading for Saint Paul's Hospital on Twentieth Street. I wanted to go there because I was sure they had seen countless stab wounds before.

Then it occurred to me that I was on bail supervision. I wasn't supposed to be out after ten o'clock.

"Take me home," I said.

"What!"

"You heard me." I raised my voice as best I could. "Take me home!"

"Don't be crazy, man! Look at you! You're hurt bad! I'll take you to the hospital." He pushed the accelerator toward the floor.

"There's going to be cops all over once I walk in. I'm supposed to be at home, so take me home. I've got a plan." The pain intensified as I spoke. I thought I was bleeding inside.

"Jesus man! You got to ..."

"Take me home!" The pain shot through me as I shouted. I could feel a numbness spreading across my torso now. The driver reluctantly asked me where I lived.

We were only half a mile from Fairhaven. It wasn't long before we pulled up in front of the apartment block where Donna and I were staying. With great difficulty, I fell out of the back seat of the Camaro. I stumbled up a flight of stairs and down the hallway. I told Donna to go ahead and phone an ambulance. I walked into the apartment and collapsed.

I lay on the floor on my back, feeling the bleeding inside me. Within minutes two large cops came barging through the door. "What happened?

I smiled uneasily. "I was showing the young lady here" — I pointed to Donna — "how to fight with knives, when" — I chuckled half-heartedly — "I walked straight into one."

The cop was no dummy. He started to write down my story, but after two sentences he raised his hands, and his voice: "This is bullshit!"

"It's true, officer," Donna started in. "It was an accident. I feel so guilty!" She covered her face with her hands.

"Bullshit!" He stared intently around the room. "All bullshit!"

The other cop, who had been looking at my wound, looked up. "Where's the knife, then?"

Donna started going through a sink full of dirty dishes. The cop stood behind her, watching her grab one after another. "I think it was this one. Or was it this one?"

I looked over at her. "I threw the knife off the balcony," I said.

The cop turned toward me. "It was an accident, officer." I smiled. "An accident."

The ambulance arrived then and the attendants started to dress the wound. I told them I could feel something flowing inside me. They radioed to the hospital that I was coming. I was expecting to be carried out on a stretcher, but the cops told them angrily to let me walk. I sat in the back of the ambulance, bent double with the pain. Then I walked into the hospital.

The wound didn't look serious. It was only three-quarters of an inch wide, but of course I couldn't tell how deep. I walked to the X-ray room. I went under some time after that. I woke up in the clothes I came in with, lying in emergency. The first person I saw was a jail guard. I thought I was under guard for breaching my bail.

"Well, well." I played it cool. "What are you doing here?"

He obviously hadn't recognized me lying there. He was taken aback. "I ... I sprained my ankle."

That was a relief. I rolled off the examining table onto my feet. I walked, bent over and very slowly, to find a bathroom. My mouth was arid. I found the bathroom and gulped down mouthfuls of water. Then I made my way back to the examination table, and with indescribable pain pulled myself back onto it. I wondered where Donna was.

A team of nurses and doctors came in and talked away in medical terminology over me. Finally, the doctor who was in charge turned toward me. "Jim, I believe you have a problem." No kidding. He pressed my abdomen. The pain was incredible. When he released his hand I almost punched him. "I believe the tube from your stomach to your bowel has been severed. We'll have to operate immediately." The nurses and doctors studied me without expression. I nodded. Immediately the doctor started giving orders for medication, operating rooms, and personnel. I was wheeled on a stretcher to X-rays. As I passed by the visiting area I saw Donna sleeping on a bench. I knew she wouldn't leave me.

I'm looking up at the team of surgeons. They put a mask on my face. "Okay, Jim, talk away," the stone-faced doctor says. I used to see this on television: the patient getting the mask over his face and the doctor asking him to count backwards from one hundred. "What you want me to talk about ... ?"

Next thing I remember I'm waking up in the recovery room. My senses are dull for a minute. I look around. There's Donna smiling away at the foot of the bed. "Hi, Neechee Moose."

"Hey, Donna." The pain reaches new heights. There is a tube running through my right nostril down to my stomach, pumping out the infectious chime. Another tube connected to a vein in my arm pumps antibiotics and fluids to sustain my body until I produce a stool for the smiling nurses, who ask me daily if I have moved my bowels. I never thought I'd be so glad to take a dump. Then the tube could be yanked out of my nose and I could taste food once again. It didn't happen for nine days.

In the hospital I get shots of pain killer every four hours. I'm so doped up that Donna beats me handily at crib on her daily visits. There is a 12 inch, semi-circular scar from my left hip to just below my sternum. It dwarfs the scar that caused all this, the puncture wound. I look pregnant. My stomach muscles have been cut in half. They take six months to regain any firmness, and it's another three months before I can attempt my first sit-up. Years afterward there is a numbness in my abdomen that will never go away, a reminder for the rest of my life of Terry Sabadash. Well Sab, I think as I struggle onto the bus in front of Saint Paul's Hospital 10 days later, I missed another Christmas, I'm scarred for life, and you're going to die.

I have no choice but to lie around the apartment. Then I have to visit the hospital, to have the dressing changed and to ask the doctor why fluid is still pouring out between the stitches. It's an infection between the skin and the muscle tissue, he says. After two weeks it clears up.

Donna and I decide to get our own apartment. While she looks around I make appointments with Welfare. There's no choice. I can't work. I can't even break the law. My stomach muscles aren't there. I have trouble getting on buses, let alone sliding through a window, or throwing people around in a downtown brawl. The Sab's death is all I can think about.

JANUARY 1986

Donna and I find a one-bedroom apartment on Avenue V, just off Twenty-Second Street. The building is full of Indians, and run by an unscrupulous landlord who is more than willing to exchange rent for sexual favors from female tenants. The building itself has been the scene of murders, rapes, suicides, assaults, and attempted murders. Why would I want to live in such a building? I'm planning to run prostitutes out of my apartment, and the crop of spaced-out tenants isn't likely to complain.

I have a pro named Juanita Sanchez, a Mexican who came to Canada five years ago to search for wealth, security, and peace, but soon discovered drugs, violence, and prostitution. She is 24. She started selling herself as a young girl in Mexico to help support her poverty-stricken family; now she does it for money and drugs. She used to work out of her girlfriend's downstairs, but that arrangement went sour when the girlfriend's mother came over to find her and an older gentlemen in their birthday suits. It's just luck that I found her when she was in search of a place to bring her regular tricks.

Juanita doesn't work regularly, just two or three tricks a week. But she has friends, and soon Linda O'Brien is bringing johns around. Linda is good. She's Irish, with flaming red hair and wild, piercing eyes. She makes up to $500 a night when she puts her mind to it. She enjoys it, too, and she gives me all the money, not like Juanita who keeps half. Linda soon becomes my favorite. I manage the money, buy her drugs and booze, and supply her with rubbers. One thing is apparent about Linda O'Brien, though: she's just as hot-headed and violent as Jimmy Tyman.

After a month of pimping and partying I find myself fighting with Linda over absolutely nothing. She swings a beer bottle by my head. I am not adept at hitting girls, but that changes instantaneously. She wheels around as I catch her with a right cross to the temple. I don't want to hit her in the face. I don't want to damage the merchandise.

"You bastard!" She tries to kick me in the balls. I block it and send her to the floor with another right cross. She jumps to her feet and then on me, scratching my face and hissing like a 130 pound cat.

I carry her to our third-floor balcony. I've made the decision. She's going head-first to the parking lot below.

"No!" Linda shrieks. I have her half over. She's clutching the railing.

"You'd better learn to fly like you can scratch, you bitch!" I'm holding her by her shins. I'm ready to let go.

"Don't, Jim!" Donna grabs me by the arms. "Please don't!"

"She's a bitch!" I shout at Donna, who is trying to pull up a shrieking Linda by the legs. Linda's arms flail wildly in the air.

"Don't, Jim!" Donna's voice is getting louder.

"Ah ..." I pull her up. Life goes on.

Linda needed to be hit once a week just to be reminded who was boss. She constantly tried to pick fights with me, scratching and kicking and punching over some trivial matter. Finally one afternoon I decided to stop this bullshit. I was driving a friend's car down Eighth Street. Linda had just pulled a trick with a regular, and I was taking her back to the apartment for another appointment.

"I want to get high," she said.

"You said you wanted to fix this john first," I reminded her.

"I do, but your bitch old lady is there. She's such a bitch. Why don't you leave that bitch?"

"I told you to leave Donna out of it." Linda and Donna never did get along. Linda was always bringing her up when we argued.

"Why doesn't she work, too? Why should that bitch get all the drugs that we buy? She's just a bitch. At least Juanita works, but your old lady gets the breaks. That's not fair."

"Linda, I'll slap you if you talk about Donna like that." I was getting steamed. I loved Donna, and I got right upset when Linda talked like this. She wanted her weekly slap, but I wasn't going to put up with this any more.

"Go ahead, tough guy! That's all you can do is hit women! You think you're so tough! Well, bullshit to that!"

It happened quickly. I was carrying a butterfly knife in my coat pocket. I leaned over and drove it into her leg. She didn't scream. She just looked at me in astonishment. The blood started to fountain out of the wound.

"Well, bitch?"

"Well what?"

"Which hospital do you want to go to?"

"Fuck the hospital!"

"Don't be a hero. I'll take you to the hospital." My voice was slow and steady. "Just don't fuck with me any more, Linda. I'll drive it into your belly next time."

"I believe you now," she replied quietly.

There were no arteries severed, no serious damage done. An hour and five stitches later we were back on the street. Linda loved me more than ever now. It started driving a wedge between Donna and me.

* * *

Linda was the main woman now. She told Juanita to hit the road and quit wasting my time. I was infuriated, and thought of knifing her again; she was interfering with my business. It all changed, though, when she handed me a gift-wrapped box. Inside was a Rolex watch and an 18 carat gold necklace.

"Now you look good, Jimmy." Her face was beaming as I fastened the $1300 watch to my wrist.

"Yeah I do, don't I." I studied the watch in the sun. I felt like a big shot.

I started selling drugs again, so money wasn't a problem.

Soon I had a 26 inch color television, a VCR, a stereo, and lots of drugs and booze. My apartment became a haven for party people. The music was loud; the people were louder. My relationship with Donna was beginning to show the strain. I was running around with Linda more then I was with Donna. When Donna brought it up I'd tell her to shut her trap or hit the road. She never left. I never really wanted her to leave. I loved her. She was my one link to sanity. Everyone else I ran with was just as insane as I was.

My stomach was healing well enough for me to start going downtown again. But this time I had a six-inch blade strapped to my belt for everyone to see. I had to use it within a week of my return downtown.

I was sitting in the bar when a young punk came up to me. "Hey Tyman, I hear you're a tough guy."

I sighed. My stomach was still three-quarters numb, and I wasn't sure if it could stand up to a fight. But I wasn't going to let on. "Better then being a waterhead like you."

His face went hard. He was small,30 pounds lighter than me, but he was going to make a name for himself downtown. "I'm no waterhead!" He grabbed a five-inch folding knife from his back pocket. "I'll cut you, fucker!"

The man was trying to intimidate me. I opened my arms and said, "Go for it now, pal, because in one second I'm going to drive this blade right into you." I patted my knife in its sheath.

He laughed. "You won't use it. You've got no balls."

I pulled out my knife. I smiled at him. He raised his, as if to get ready for a fight. He was still thinking I was going to back down. I passed the knife between my left and right hands in front of his face. When I saw his eyes transfixed on the movement, I drove the knife into his leg. It went completely through.

"Jesus, Jim!" It was a hooker who knew me. "Settle down." She gave me a disgusted look. The guy was still in shock. People milled around. Someone tied a belt around his thigh to stop the bleeding. They arranged to get him to a hospital.

"I'm going to shoot you, Tyman," he mumbled as he was helped out of the bar. "I'm going to shoot you."

I walked up to him.

"Forget it!" It was the same hooker. "C'mon Jim, drop it already!" Her voice was getting angry. I looked at her. She was my friend and I got along with her cousins pretty well. I said to him, "I'll drop it, pal. But don't ever think I'm going to roll over again." I walked away.

I was hotter then hell now. I went looking for old scores to settle. Sab came to mind. I didn't find him that night, but I tracked him down to a bar in another part of town. I took Linda along.

"Okay Linda, you go in and tell him you're in trouble. Tell him you need his help with a couple of guys. He thinks he's a real macho man, anyway. He'll come to your rescue, and that's when I'll get him."

Linda nodded uneasily. She liked to see me get rank, but this was beyond her limits. I had no limits any more. She wanted to please me and at the same time protect me, so she made her own plans when she walked in.

I sat in the car and waited ... and waited. Finally I packed my knife and went inside. Linda was sitting down. When she saw me, she jumped up and ran to the corner of the bar, behind a partition. Baffled, I followed her. I heard her outraged voice, and came around the partition in time to see her slash Sab's forearm; he had raised it to protect his face. She tried again for his face. He jumped back with fear in his eyes. The screaming started then. Bartenders raced over. I grabbed Linda by the waist and carried her out while she cursed at the terrified Sab. We got out the back door, jumped in the car, and roared away.

Linda started laughing. "See that bastard's eyes light up when he saw my knife?" She laughed harder. Then she filled me in on her own plan: "I don't want to lose you, Jimmy. I'll get that bastard for you. Just give me time, I'll get him for you." Linda was in love with me.

After that incident Sab was rumored to have gone up north.

Revenge was put on hold. I still had a robbery charge to face in June. On a visit to my lawyer I finally learned what had happened. A woman and her companions had got beaten up, and had their purses and two cases of beer stolen. When my lawyer told me the facts and the dates, it all fell into place. A buddy of mine had played "football" with this woman. It's a game they often play on Twentieth Street. The player spots an older woman, or in this case a fat woman, with a case of beer. He races up behind her, knocks her to the ground, and takes her beer. They he yells "Fumble!" and runs away. But it doesn't always work out that way. This woman had companions. The companions gave chase. My buddy had companions, too. They chased after the chasers. When everyone caught everyone else, a brawl ensued. That's when I came strolling by with Donna. I was pointed out as one of the muggers, and for some reason I was the only one arrested. It happened a month after I got out of jail, and I wasn't arrested till the night of the shooting in the Baldwin. Almost a year after the alleged crime I was finally heading for my preliminary hearing.

I strolled into court. It had been almost a year since I got out of jail, and the only contact I'd had with the police lately was from a distance. One night three months before I'd been out on my balcony when I noticed a man watching the building from across the street. I realized that my apartment and myself were under surveillance. I asked Linda to go ask him up for a beer. He declined, of course, but I wanted to see how fast his backup could get there. A white Cordoba roared up within seconds. So the game continued. He would switch off with another undercover officer. They didn't have a schedule, or pattern, but every time they came by to watch, I waved to them. Sometimes one of them would wave back.

I sat in the courtroom alone. I'd been partying the night away and had yet to go to sleep. I was yawning as my lawyer explained that the woman was willing to drop the charge of robbery if I pleaded guilty to common assault. I roared back at him: "I never touched the woman! All I did was walk by as she was fighting with three other women and her friends were fighting with three guys. I never touched anyone!"

"Jim, it's a good deal. With your record, you'll be committed to trial, and then who knows what will happen?" He shrugged his shoulders and lifted his eyebrows. "What do you say?'

I was mad. I cursed the justice system and said, "All right, go for it. You'll get me a fine, right?"

"No problem, Jim. I've already talked to the prosecutor about it."

I watch him strut around in front of the judge's podium. He was joking with the prosecutor. "I've already talked to the prosecutor about it." His words echoed in my mind. I cursed softly. I looked around the courtroom. The complainant was there, not looking at me. I wanted to go up and ask her why she was charging me. Damn cops probably made her charge me, I thought.

Donna walked in and sat beside me. "I told you I wanted to come." She spoke softly.

"You were sleeping," I said, "so I left you alone."

"Well, you should have woken me up." She looked at me pleadingly. "C'mon Jim, you know how much I care for you."

I studied her expression. I felt like a world-class jerk. She was so wonderful to me, and I was running around with a hooker who was willing to die for me. Linda's motives were unclear. I knew Donna would die for me, too, but it was love that motivated her. I thought of my family. They'd had that same look. I had to turn away from her. It hurt too much.

I received a $400 fine for common assault. It was almost funny. The year since I'd got out of jail had been the most violent and criminally active year of my life, and now I had just received my first conviction for a violent offense — for something I didn't do. Donna and I left the courthouse and walked across to the Baldwin Hotel. I was officially unrestricted, so it was a good enough reason to kick up our heels. We went into the bar and I ordered doubles for the next hour.

"Jim," Donna said softly, "I know I can't tell you what to do, but why don't you settle down now? You said you were going to look for your real family. I'll help you along if you want."

I studied her expression. She was truly concerned. Why? The Tymans were concerned, too. I know that now. Again, why? "Why do you care?" I asked her, stone-faced.

"Oh c'mon sweetheart!" Donna sounded exasperated. She was obviously annoyed with the question.

"I've got money. I can buy you drugs and booze. That's why you stick around, right?" My voice rose as I spoke.

"Sure, Jim!" Donna doesn't get mad often, but she was now. "Do you remember all the things you said to me when you were in jail? Over the phone?"

"No, I don't remember!"

"Remember the letter you wrote to me when you were in Secure? About your biological family, and how it's bothered you all your life?"

I had to think for a minute. "Yeah, I remember. But that was before. Things are different now."

"What's so different?" Donna demanded. "Remember, you said you thought your family was me, then you thought your family was pimps and whores, and that you'd never be involved in such a thing. You said you were an apple once and now you're a proud Indian. You won't become like the Indians you see downtown, killing themselves over nothing."

She let it all sink in. I did remember telling her those things over the phone. It was true, I didn't believe I would become a pimp. And really, I'd been so close to killing someone — over what? But like in the past, when I felt cornered by my conscience, I reacted aggressively. "Who gives a fuck! These bastards are goofs anyway! And besides, Donna, what can I do? Who's going to hire a big Indian? Would you want a big fuckin' Indian or a pretty boy honky working for you? Well, Donna?" I raised my voice enough that the early morning drunks turned their heads toward us.

Donna must have rehearsed this. "Has the big fuckin' Indian ever tried?" she asked coolly.

I was going to answer back quickly, but I was tongue-tied. I tried one more excuse: "I was going to, but I got stabbed, so I couldn't work. And besides, Donna, I'm an ex-con. Who wants an ex-con, and an Indian besides?"

"Proud Indians aren't disgraced by their race." She was so composed.

Again, she had me. I was going to say I'm not disgraced, but I couldn't. If it was anyone else but the girl I loved saying I was disgraced I'd be leaning across the table with my hands wrapped neatly and tightly around her throat. I answered her softly: "But the honkies, Donna. They're so racist! It makes me sick."

"I know, Jim. But they're not all like that. The bad ones have a lot of influence, but there are some who don't say, `Oh, here comes another Indian, probably wants a handout.'" She deepened her voice and chuckled to herself. I laughed with her. I remembered Calvin telling me the same things. It was sinking in now.

"You're right, Donna, but there so many of the bastards."

"Yeah, there are, but don't let their ignorance kill you. You're rank and violent because you're so damn mad about being Indian. Don't let them win."

"What do you mean, don't let them win!?"

"By killing yourself or killing someone else you'll let them know that you were just another rank Indian." She paused for a moment. "You're helping them hate you, Neechee Moose."

I was off balance. She was right, then she was wrong. It was the honkies' fault, it was the government's fault, it was the Indians' fault. Maybe it's everyone's fault?

"Donna?"

"Yeah."

"How come you're so smart? You're just a squaw!"

She gave me a cocky grin. "Well, at least it's better then being an FBI."

"FBI?" I was puzzled.

"Fuckin' Big Indian!" She laughed.

We kept on talking. I told her I would look for my family, and even try to find a job. My link to sanity was stronger then I had foreseen. I grew closer to her that day.

I got a job clearing brush along the river bank. It was a program set up by the government for welfare cases who had no job skills and no work experience worth mentioning. It was a start, Donna said. I replied angrily that I'd been raking in thousands a month from crime; why should I bust my ass for a bunch of honkies? I didn't get the way I was overnight, and I wasn't going to change overnight. Because my old friends were out of jail, and Linda came up with a lucrative idea, I was back into it after two weeks of attempting to go straight.

I found myself in possession of $30,000 worth of jewelry. Jewelry sells easily on the street. Linda had a drug dealer and a foolproof plan to burn him, so one night we did exactly that. Now I was in possession of 300 tablets of speeders. I started fixing speed. I was fixing everyone who came over to our apartment. I started taking Donna downtown more than ever. I took her to restaurants. I bought her a fur coat, a few clothes. I kept her drunk and stoned as much as possible. I didn't want her to try to straighten me out again. Crime was too lucrative and too easy.

The partying picked up speed. I was fixing teeze regularly; they're like winnies only stronger. It started running up to $100 a day, then $200. I justified it by telling Donna that I wasn't drinking as much now. But finally the stares and disappointed looks got to me, so with smooth talk and kisses I convinced her to fix along with me. I had things in control again. I had one pro and two part-timers pulling tricks out of my apartment. The police were always outside, watching. We continued waving to each other. I bought another car. I was cruising once again, because life was great, I was full of hate.

I had a friend who used to drive Linda to meet her johns when I wasn't available. One day he went to pick her up at a place on Avenue H. I didn't like going there. A guy who lived there I'd known as a Protective Custody case in the Regina

Correctional Center, and I was having nothing to do with waterheads. A homosexual and a lesbian were living there, too, along with the PC case's sister, with whom the PC case was having an incestuous relationship. It was a situation any deviant would cherish.

A fight broke out between the homosexual and the lesbian over who should do the laundry. My friend decided to referee. He ended up struggling on the floor with Ken, the homosexual, who pulled a knife and stabbed him. My friend managed to get out alive. He came over to my place, stitched and asking for revenge. I was over there with a car-load of ruffians within an hour.

When half a dozen people walked in, everyone knew what was up. Ken started stating his case immediately: it wasn't my friend's beef, he shouldn't have got involved. I smiled at him. "You like beef, don't you?"

He was sitting on the couch, frightened and meek, when Linda waltzed in. Her eyes said there was going to be trouble. She said hello to everyone, cool as you please. She asked for the butterfly knife I had stabbed her with months ago. I wasn't sure what she was up to.

"Hi, Ken."

"Hi, Linda."

Linda walked up to him, and started showing him how to use the butterfly knife. She flipped it around in her hands while Ken sat wide-eyed, nodding meekly through it all. Then she drove it into his thigh, severing an artery and chipping his thigh bone. "There you go, you bastard! Stab my friend, eh!" She calmly turned and handed back the bloodied knife.

The PC case had a knife beside him. He jumped up and put it to my throat. "You bastards leave or Tyman gets it!"

"Fuck you, asshole!" I swore at him.

"You think I'm a PC case, Tyman?" He asked excitedly. I could smell glue on his breath. I had different thoughts now that I knew his mind was soaked in Lepage's Contact Cement. Besides being a PC case, he was a gluehead.

"Nah, you're no PC case." I was composed. I hoped he didn't have the balls to slit my throat, but glueheads are unpredictable.

"I'm not a PC case! I'm solid, Tyman! I'm no bug! I'm solid!" His breath was giving me a headache.

I didn't answer him. I stood there feeling the blade of the knife press into my larynx. If he'd known what I was thinking he would probably have started slicing. But he released me and backed himself against the wall, all the time going on about how solid a guy he was and if I wanted to fuck with him I could come to his place any time. He moved like a cat, holding the knife in front of him, alert for any movement. He got to the door and darted out. He was gone from sight within a minute.

Meanwhile Ken sat clutching his thigh. The blood was pouring out like a faucet. The wound was serious. He was in the hospital two weeks. He lost muscles in his leg, and limped for four months. He charged Linda, but he refused to testify against her after he was given a quiet talk in a back alley one night. She claimed self-defense and got 90 days. If she hadn't already admitted to stabbing him she might have got off with nothing.

The gluehead was dealt with soon after. One night his house was burglarized and vandalized, and his television and VCR were stolen. After that he apologized to me for his "uncharacteristic behavior," as he put it. I accepted. After all, being a gluehead is misery enough.

My drug habit was getting expensive. So was the way I wanted to live. I had a habit of buying people drinks in the bars I frequented. The bill would run as high as $500 a night, so I put more demands on Linda. She was getting upset. I had never pushed her before to make money. But now things were picking up. I had a car, and the gas was running $100 a week. Welfare was paying the rent and a few groceries. Pimping was paying for the parties and drugs. Donna started to bring up my drug use again. I pointed to the tracks on her arm, and she fell silent. I lay awake at night, or sat on my balcony watching the undercover cop across the street sipping his coffee and eating his doughnuts, wondering where to go. I was thinking of expanding the prostitution business. I had a few girls in mind. They were Linda's friends, and they feared and respected me— necessary requirements in the pimping business. I was going to get into escorting: advertise them in the papers, just like used cars.

I wanted more. I decided to break the rule I had set a year ago when I started all this. I decided to put my sacred Donna out on the street.

It happened at Linda's apartment one night. Where the two of them once didn't get along, now they joined forces to try to stop my runaway life. They both loved me in different ways. They were at Linda's that night when I came back from the bar. I was wired, and I had a plan.

"C'mon Linda, I need some money. Let's go." I said as soon as I walked through the door.

Linda and Donna were at the kitchen table, drinking coffee. Donna spoke first: "Why don't you stay away from downtown tonight? Pick up some beer and let's play cards or something." They were going to try to slow me down first, then get the needle away from me.

"Fuck the cards! We're young and free. Let's party!" I looked at Donna for a moment. "You get ready, too," I said.

"What?" She had an astonished look.

"Yeah, c'mon. You can pull a few tricks."

She stood up. "Are you serious?"

"Why not?"

"You said you never wanted me out there. You wanted me for yourself."

"You love me, don't you?"

Donna was aghast. She turned away and spoke softly. "Yes, I love you, but you said you never wanted me out there."

"Who's paying for your drugs? Who's paying for the parties? It sure as hell ain't you! Now you get a chance to feel important, so c'mon!"

Linda watched in astonishment. She jumped in. "Forget it, Jim. I'll go. Leave Donna out of it."

"Fuck that bullshit! Donna, you're coming too! You're going to pay your own way from now on!"

"No!" She turned toward me. "I don't want to live this way any more! It's ... it's just wrong, Jim! We're killing ourselves. You've changed since you got out!" Her eyes were wide with hurt and anger.

"Ah, fuck you then, tramp!" She hated that word and I knew it. She tried to slap me. I floored her with a straight right to the forehead. Linda came to her rescue.

"Jim, don't hit her!"

I didn't even blink. I pulled my knife and slashed Linda across the forearm. She clutched her arm. But she was a scrapper. She shot into her bedroom and came out with a knife high and ready. "You bastard! You cut me, I'll show you!" She stabbed for my stomach. I side-stepped her and drove her once in the side of the head. Then I grabbed her by the hair and pulled her back to the kitchen table. I had her bent over backwards, the knife at her throat. Her own knife lay on the carpet. Suddenly her eyes were expressionless, her voice the same. "Go ahead, kill me. I can't take it any more. I want to die from you, not someone else. Please do it."

Donna jumped on my back. Her voice was hysterical and pleading at the same time. "Don't Jim! Jesus Christ Jim! Look at what's happening! Please Jim, just look!"

I stood up so fast that Donna went flying. She fell to the ground. She grabbed Linda's knife. She was on her haunches, sobbing and clutching the knife.

"Are you going to stab me, Donna?" I asked coolly.

She was trying to muffle her sobs. "Please Jim, don't, don't please." She was near hysteria.

I walked toward her. She moved back, and kept moving back into a corner. She was sobbing.

"C'mon, Donna. Use it. I'm coming, Donna."

"Don't, please," she said between sobs.

I booted the knife out of her hand. She screamed. She raised her hands to protect her face. My knife sliced her forearm. Blood spurted out, and my heart dropped. I couldn't believe what I had done. I turned and ran out the door.

I went to a party of pimps and pros. I drank whisky from the bottle. I fixed teeze and purchased a dozen from the dealer. I started a fight with another pimp. The knives came out. He kept pleading with me; he wanted nothing to do with this maniac. I got him three times: in the liver, the lung, and the arm. I'd have murdered him if my friends hadn't grabbed the knife from my hand.

The party lasted a week. I never went home. I didn't know where Donna was. I didn't phone her or inquire at the hospitals. I tried to drink away my guilt. I tried to fix it away. It wouldn't leave. I decided a week later to go home. I had one last hurrah planned.

I was 24 now, and I'd lived a life beyond description. I frequented bars that I used to mock as a kid. I had taken to pimping. I had destroyed relationships with my family, who loved and cared for me: their only wish was to see me live happily. And now this. I had frightened Donna beyond anything she would ever experience. That wasn't the plan I had when I saw this beautiful 15 year old in an arcade, playing Pac-Man.

I crushed the teeze up. I was going to die tonight.

PART THREE

Recovery

Teeze was $15 a pill at that time. You crushed four or five and mixed them with warm water, and if your tolerance wasn't up it was enough to stop your heart, to stop your life. I was going to make sure. Lucky seven was my number. I'd once done four; it made my hands vibrate and my insides erupt. I never went under, but I knew that was the limit. I knew if I ever crossed that line it would be the end, tragic. But now I didn't even think of it being tragic. I'd be helping the cops out by overdosing. They wouldn't see it as a tragedy. They'd greet the news with smiles and a sense of relief. I got the cigarette filter ready.

I had a three-cc needle which I usually filled up halfway when I shot up two teeze. With seven I'd use the whole capacity of the needle. It was a fatal dose, to say the least. But what the hell, no use pussy-footing around.

I had the empty pill container ready, then I realized I didn't need a cigarette filter for teeze. I must have been confused; it was the talwins you needed the filter for. I unscrewed the needle from the rig and put the barrel to the bottom of the pill bottle. I pulled the plunger up. I watched the white liquid rise until it filled the barrel, then I screwed the needle back on.

I had scars from shooting up, and I used them to find a vein. Most of them were collapsed. I had to tie my arm to get them to the surface. Finally I found a vein, tiny and frail. I fumbled with it as it moved about under the skin. I felt the sweat forming on my brow. Then I saw blood enter the barrel of the rig and I started feeding the fluid into my arm. It was working. I could feel the ether engulf my air passages. I watched the liquid descend with the push of the plunger. Then it was gone, and so was I.

I felt the rush coming. It was more than I could handle. I threw up over the kitchen table. I dropped the needle as I struggled to stand, then I staggered about, knocking over chairs, knocking over pots from the kitchen cabinet. I threw up again. My vision faded as the room started to spin. My head felt detached. I saw whiteness, blinding. I thought I saw Donna, but I couldn't be sure. I fell face-first on the kitchen table, then dropped to the floor. I felt warm blood running over my face. It seemed so peaceful now, I thought, I smiled, I felt like sleeping now ...

I'm floating. I hear Donna talking, but I can't understand what she's saying. I feel that I'm floating around the apartment. My face feels wet and cold. Donna is talking to me, and she's throwing water on my face. If Donna is here I'm still alive.

"C'mon, Tyman! You bastard, wake up! Help me!" She's shouting in my face. I can feel cold water running down my chest and into my mouth, my nostrils, my eyes.

"You fuckin' big Indian! Move! Get up! Walk with me! You stupid bastard! Help me!"

Donna, I can hear you. Why are you yelling? My face begins to sting. She's slapping me, back and forth. "Quit slapping me." I'm sure it was me who talked. She slaps me again. "I said quit slapping me!" I feel angry.

"Get up and do something about it then!" Donna's voice, then a hard slap. "C'mon, tough guy! Get up and straighten out your old lady!" More slapping. "C'mon, bastard! Chicken! Goof! Get up, asshole!" She slaps me some more.

I'm pissed off. I get up as fast as I can, and fall back a lot faster. I'm on my hands and knees. "C'mon, asshole! I'm right here! Hit me!" She's yelling in my ear. You bitch, you're damn right I'm going to hit you, as soon as I can get to my feet.

"You gotta ... you gotta problem, bitch?" I talk slowly. My balance is gone. I still feel detached, like it's a dream.

"C'mon, Tyman! Come here! Follow me!"

I look through a fog at Donna. She has her arm in a sling. She slaps me again, and throws more water in my face. I feel as if I'm looking through a dirty window.

"C'mon goofball! Follow me!"

You don't call someone a goof unless you mean to fight him. I follow her. I'm going to punch her in that smart-ass mouth of hers.

"That's it, keep coming." She continues taunting me. "Let's go outside and fight. That way we won't break any of this cheap furniture you bought! Fuckin' goof, can't even buy good furniture! Spend all your money on Barbie Dolls so you can play with something in the bathroom. Hey, Tyman! C'mon, goof, outside! I'll kick your ass out there!" She walks out the door.

"Bitch!" I follow. I fall against the door. "You mouthy bitch! Come here! Call me a goof, hey! Come here!" I stumble out the door, walk toward her. "I thought you wanted to fight." I grab for her. She steps back easily.

"What's going on?" It's Ray from downstairs, the caretaker.

"Jim's overdosed," Donna answers quickly. "Help me keep him moving."

Overdose? I don't remember anything like that. Ray grabs me under the arm. "C'mon Jim, let's go for a walk." He struggles to keep me up while Donna throws more water in my face.

It's late November, and the pair of them are throwing snow and water in my face. Ray's wife is there now, too. I'm being helped along as we walk around and around the parking lot. People are coming out on their balconies and asking what I did to myself this time. Soon they just offer advice: "Keep him moving." So they do. I have brief moments of coherence when I demand to know what's going on. Then I slip away again. I feel as if my face is freezing. It is. But Donna throws more water when she sees my eyes roll back. My body convulses; the walk continues.

Later they told me that I tried to fight with everyone. I was egged on by Donna, Ray, his wife. They told me it was the only thing that kept me up when I was slipping away — being challenged to a fight.

"Are you okay now?"

I'm coherent, anyway. I'm leaning against the building. Ray's wife is bringing me coffee, shaking her head. Ray is smiling away. "You overdid it with the teeze, eh buddy?" His laugh is too deep and too loud to come from his body. "Yeah I did, didn't I?" I fake a smile. Donna looks at me suspiciously. She knows, but she smiles anyway. She won't shame me. She's wearing a sling. Her tendons were severed when I slashed her. She'll need therapy to regain the full use of her hand. I feel more terrible when I hear that, but she laughs when I apologize. "Don't worry about it, Neechee Moose. You were loaded." She smiles at me.

"You're crazy, Jim," Ray comments, then lets out a cloud of steam with his big boisterous laugh.

You're right, pal. Just plain fuckin' crazy." I look at Donna. We exchange looks that are filled with the pain and the shame of the past week. "Sorry, Donna." I smile at her. "I'm sorry."

"Forget about it already! Just don't do it again, or you can walk yourself around this parking lot." She laughs.

CHRISTMAS 1986

I finally spend a Christmas on the street, my first since 1982. Donna makes a dinner like I haven't experienced since childhood, when my mother used to cook a huge turkey for as many as 20 people. We even have guests. There are six of us, but I'm the only man. I get the honor of slicing the bird.

I have given up fixing, and selling drugs. I still drink, and use marijuana, but like I said, you don't get this way overnight, so you don't quit overnight. I still have Linda pulling tricks out of the apartment. But the good news for Christmas is the fact that

I found myself a job. Donna and I are happier now. We go out to movies and restaurants more. I'm trying to live straight and peaceful, and it's happening. I tell Donna that we'll move and then I'll quit pimping and work full time. She just says she's happy. She doesn't care how I make money, as long as I never get that way again. She thought of leaving me. She didn't really know why she decided to come home that night. She just thought she had to. I'm glad she did.

Donna and I move to the east side of Saskatoon. I love it already. There are hardly any cops around. We have a basement suite, so our two cats can go outside all the time. I have a job in an auto body shop. It's part of a work program set up by the John Howard Society, with financial backing from the government. It's designed to give ex-cons like me a shot at working. It's a great idea, I have to admit. Without a program like that, I don't know what I'd have done.

So life is going well. I hardly bother with Linda now. She still comes over, but talk about prostitution doesn't come up. She's planning to attend adult upgrading classes through the Community College. Donna has a job in a women's clothing store in Midtown Plaza downtown, and appears quite pleased with it. She always brings up this straight-john life we're living. "Next thing we'll be going to community teas together," she laughs.

I've been out of jail for 21 and a half months. I've decided to take a leave of absence from work. The boss warns me that my job may not be here when I come back. But it's something I have to do, something I need to know, to understand more about myself. I ask the Native Alcohol Center if they can put me through their 30 day program. They agree. I'm scheduled for May 18th to June 18th, 1987. I'm going in for treatment.

It was during this time that I found my real mother. I asked a fellow ex-con one day. He looked at me strangely for a minute after I told him my story, then he stretched out his hand and said, "Howdy, Cuz."

"What?"

"If Alice is your mother, and it sounds like she is, and if Randy's my cousin, which he is, then you must be also. Hi, cuz."

I was stunned. I'd been in jail with this guy plenty; to think he was my cousin blew me away. But I carried the information with me, and told street people about it, and they agreed to call me when they saw Randy or my mother in the bars. Then one day it happened: I got word she was sitting in the Barry Hotel on Twentieth and B. I felt like throwing up when I walked through that door and saw her sitting there. She didn't know I was coming.

She was shocked — understandably — when I stood in front of her and her new husband and told her I was her son from 18 years ago. She asked me my name twice. She looked at me. She looked at her husband, who was in a fog over all this. She looked back at me. She was wearing dark glasses, so I couldn't see her eyes. But I did see the tears slide down from behind the glasses. It was true, she was my mother. I held her while she sobbed, fighting my own tears.

She told me of my years of abuse at the hands of a Frenchman who drank too much and hit me too much. It led to their divorce. I had more brothers and sisters. Only Randy and I had got into trouble with the law. Another brother was making $35,000 a year, honestly. I was the last of her children. She never forgot about me, but she never dreamed she would ever see me again. Neither did I. She gave me her phone number and address. I never did phone her or go by her house on Thirty-Third Street. Her new husband wanted me to call him "Pop." I shook my head. I had a father, he died a long time ago.

I walked in the park by the river with Donna and told her about my meeting with my mother. She asked if I was going to look for my real brothers and sisters now. I didn't answer her. I didn't know. I had found my mom, but it wasn't the meeting it was supposed to be. I don't know what I was expecting, but I was growing up. I was aware now of who was really my real mom: Cecile Tyman, the one who raised me, fed me, and loved me. It was wrong to think Alice was going to take over. I'd been lost all my life, but finding my biological mother wasn't going to change the way I lived. I realized that. It took some scary moments, some hurt moments, but I still had Donna, and I was making contact with the Tymans more frequently.

During my 30 day stay at the Native Alcohol Center I learned more than ever. They had a saying, a philosophy: "Drinking is not the problem, living is the problem." I was an alcoholic; there was no disputing that. But I was trying to learn how to live with myself, not how to quit drinking.

I finished the program and continued sober for two weeks before I started drinking again. All I cared about was that I was proud to be Indian. I was glad I'd completed the 30-day program. I learned a lot about myself, and I learned a lot about Indians from up north, who seem to show up in crowds for the NAC program. They told me stories about Lysol parties when they were 10 years old, and how it just kept on going. They were burnt out when I talked to them, and most of them were around 20 years old. I felt sad for them. Life appeared to be over for them. They would come back to the NAC again and again to dry out, get healthy, and tackle life one more time.

I started looking for another job. I had a line on one down on the riverbank, cutting brush — the same job I'd had for two weeks last year. I was going to start the first of August, 1987. It wasn't the job I wanted, but it had to do. Donna and I were just making ends meet. I still had a lot of friends into prostitution and drugs, but I was keeping myself clean. The temptation was great in the beginning when I was first attempting the straight-john life, but over the past few months I had even stopped carrying knives. I was feeling relaxed and secure with my life. I was glad I'd found my mother and my forgotten past, and had decided to look for my brothers and sisters in the coming months, just to see what had happened to them. And boy was I glad that Donna had the courage to come back that night. She was planning to go to school in the fall, and we were going to move closer to downtown since I finally blew red on the breathalyzer one night and was about to lose my license. But even that didn't bother me. I was just happy and content with myself. Then I went to the wrong party. Donna stayed home the night I decided to go see my old buddies down at the Barry Hotel. We all went to the party together. I met a good-looking girl who offered to work for me. I was drunk. I decided to take her to see Donna, to see if she would approve. Why, I don't know. But if Donna said yes, I was going for it. We walked by a convenience store, and this girl ran up to the glass doors and kicked them in. I stood and watched as she dumped cartons and cartons of smokes into a shopping bag. My gut was turning over.

I awoke to a pounding on the door by two police officers. I motioned for Donna to answer it and say I'm not home. I knew what it was about.

I went downtown that night, and took Donna with me. I could feel the heat closing in. A fire broke out in the bar that night, and the place was evacuated. I stood outside drinking beer and a cop with a smile pasted in place came up to me. "You're under arrest, Tyman." I was led away, handcuffed, and placed in the back seat of the cruiser, charged with breaking and entering.

The store had a video camera and I showed up on the tape, standing out front drinking beer. Since I was known to the police, I was identified immediately and a warrant was issued the next morning. My accomplice couldn't be identified.

"Tell us who your female partner is, Jim, and we'll drop the charge. By the picture, we can tell you were just watching, but that's good enough for aiding and abetting. Good enough in your case, anyway. So come on, Jim. Scratch our backs and we'll scratch yours." A cocky smile graced his kisser. I wanted to hit it.

I smiled at him. "I know fuck-all, copper!"

"It's probably one of your whores, right? Which one, Linda? Or your old lady, Donna? Yeah, it was probably Donna. We'll go pick up Donna, that's what we'll do. Or should we?" He showed me his grin again.

"Fuck you, asshole. It wasn't Donna!"

"Fuck you, Tyman. You're going to jail."

It was July 31st, 1987. I was thrown into the city cells for the long weekend, three days and three nights. I lay in my gym shorts, thinking of the real progress I had made before all this. I knew who it was, but it didn't enter my mind to pull a Judas. I know Donna wasn't thinking about it, either. I wondered if the cops were going to follow up on their threat. Of course they would. It's part of the game.

I wake up sore and cold; the city only gives you a see-through sheet to cover yourself. I don't eat the Egg McMuffin the city supplies for breakfast. My guts are churning. I wonder what sentence this will bring. I've been out for over two years, but that won't mean a thing. The cops have been on my ass for the past year. I'm history. They've got me in their cage and they aren't going to open the door for a long time.

I use the phone to call Donna. It's about nine o'clock in the morning. I wait and wait while the phone rings and rings in our basement suite. No one answers. I give back the phone. I shout: "Donna! Hey, Donna!"

"Yeah!" Donna shouts back from the women's holding cells. "Nice meeting you here."

Donna told me they came busting in about two o'clock in the morning, searched the place and of course found nothing, and placed her under arrest for breaking and entering.

A justice of the peace came around about ten o'clock in the morning, either to release people or to remand them till Tuesday morning, when the judge can decide what to do with them. I was expecting to be remanded, but I wasn't expecting to hear this: "You have also been charged with arson, to wit, the Barry Hotel." I glared at the wrinkled old JP. The scrawny young cop stood smiling. He would have started giggling, but he bit down on his finger to stop. What a fine man to marry someone's daughter, so they can have kids just like him.

I smiled back. I was not going to show it, but I was rattled and I was upset. I felt like throwing up. Then I regained my composure, and I started to laugh. I'm sure the kid in the next cell thought I was cracking up. I knew it was another bogus beef. I was going to beat the rap, not only that rap but four other bum raps the JP remanded me for — all bogus, all maneuvers by the police.

They made their next move in the middle of the night.

"Jim, Jim." It was a cop I knew well. He'd been on my ass for the past six months. He was banging the bars lightly with his flashlight.

"What do you want?" I asked groggily. I was finally getting a decent sleep, and now this.

"What about these ARs around town, Jim? What can you say about them?" It was three, four in the morning, and he stood smiling away. He wanted to talk.

I rolled onto my side. "I know fuck-all, copper."

"Think, Jimmy. You've got a break and enter, plus those other charges to worry about. You could be looking at a long time." He added smoothly, "Or, as your type of people say, we might swing a deal." He hooked his thumbs in his belt and rocked back on his heels. I was waiting for him to start whistling softly. It would have suited the image he was projecting.

"You're a real prince, aren't you?" I turned onto my back, put my hands behind my head. This guy was good. I wanted to string him along for a while. "What about Donna?"

"That will be our first good deed, Jimmy. Tell us something, and Donna goes home to feed your cats." His smile was as shiny as his badge.

"What's this bullshit arson charge?"

"Well, you know, Jimmy" — he stretched out his hands — "someone makes a complaint, we have to investigate." He smiled brightly. "It's bullshit, Jimmy, but we hold the aces all the time."

"I see." I nodded my head. "Well, the guy who held up the store is still around town."

He moved closer to the bars. "Yeah? Who is he?"

"Sshh, pal." I motioned with my eyes to the next cells. "You don't want to blow my cover, do you?"

"No, no. Sorry, Jim. Well, where can I find him?"

"My place."

The cop had a dumbfounded look. "Your place?"

"Yeah, his name is Bennie."

"What's he look like?" He pulled out his notebook to jot down the description.

"Well, he has green eyes, a very dark complexion, and four legs." I muffled a laugh.

The cop shot a glance at me. "What the fuck are you talking about?"

"Bennie is my cat. They call him a cat burglar. But occasionally he holds up convenience stores when he needs a fix of catnip. You know how it is, eh copper?"

He kept his composure. "See you in '89, Jimmy." He walked away.

It was two years till 1989. That meant the cop was going to talk to the prosecutor and ask for three years.

I was whisked off to the remand unit of the Saskatoon Correctional Center. I had eight criminal charges against me: two counts of break and enter, two counts of mischief, one count of impaired driving, one count of possession of stolen property, one count of possession of stolen license plates, and one count of arson. I was planning on pleading guilty in September to four of them. The rest I was going to beat in court.

I was denied bail as expected, but so was Donna. She went to a higher court, and bail was set at $500 for the breaking and entering charge. One week after she was released on bail, the prosecutor phoned her lawyer to inform him the charge would be dropped. And so it was, without trial or preliminary hearing.

On September 21st, 1987, I was sentenced to two years less a day in the Saskatoon Correctional Center. I had four other charges to face in the coming months. I beat them all. I knew I would. I knew they were bogus, but it was part of the cops' plan to manipulate me into being their spy. It didn't work and they knew it. So I received two years for watching a crime. Justice had been done.

I will have spent another 18 months behind bars when I get out. The jail is the same: skinners and stool pigeons are given VIP status, hardcore inmates are shunned and ignored. I have a new attitude this time, though. The hatred is gone. The shame of being Indian is not there. The thought of living by crime once I get out isn't there. I make contact with the Tymans more often. Donna is glad for me. She can see the difference on our visits. Instead of me talking about stabbing and robbing people, I talk about school and careers. She smiles at me throughout a visit. Finally I get annoyed enough to ask her what she's smiling about.

"Oh, just you. You're going to make it, Tyman. I know you are. I can tell." Then she hugs me.

"I know, Donna. I will make it. My gut feelings tell me that."

About the Author and the Book

James Tyman returned to the Saskatoon Correctional Center on September 21, 1987. He was sentenced to two years less a day. Shortly after his sentence began, James started to write. His first attempts concentrated on crime fiction, but eventually he shifted his efforts to his own story. Once he did so he completed *Inside Out* in six weeks. He was twenty four years old.

On December 17, 1988 Jim was released from jail. Through the John Howard Society he attended an institute to study autobody repair. This past spring he began working and he has applied to attend university where he hopes to eventually study journalism or law. He has taken on the job of rebuilding his life against incredible odds. All of us at Fifth House Publishers are privileged to have had the opportunity to work and be friends with this very courageous young man.

In Jim's words "*Inside Out* was not written to seek pity nor was it done to ask forgiveness. I wrote this book to simply ask for understanding and acceptance for myself and all Native people."

Printed in Canada